The Ohio Bridge

HARRY R. STEVENS

The Ohio Bridge
CINCINNATI'S ROEBLING
SUSPENSION BRIDGE
1846-1939

COMMONWEALTH BOOK COMPANY
St. Martin, Ohio

Copyright © 1939 by The Covington and Cincinnati Bridge Company. Copyright © 2020 by Commonwealth Book Company. Printed in the United States of America. Title Page Photograph: John A. Roebling.

ISBN: 978-1-948986-16-8

I for one would say, do not obstruct "La belle riviere"—there is but one in the world —*John A Roebling*, 1846.

Posterity will find no satisfaction, and but little justification, in this, for the accumulation of injury which . . . must result to Cincinnati, to Ohio, to the Union, from any such work as is now proposed.—*Remarks Upon Mr. Roebling's "Plan and Report . . .,"* 1847.

It is scarcely deemed necessary to say to you that the Bridge is a complete success.—*Board of Directors*, 1867.

THE history of the bridge is full of romance. Many men have given their all so that it may render a real public service. People may wonder how or why it was built, and it occurred to us that this record may become useful to those who are interested.

CONTENTS

	PAGE
THE RIVER	1
IN NEED OF A BRIDGE	4
EARLY PLANS AND BRIDGES	9
FROM TALK TO ACTION	12
JOHN A. ROEBLING	17
CHARLES ELLET	26
THE COVINGTON AND CINCINNATI BRIDGE COMPANY	29
THE FIRST ROUND	35
ROEBLING'S REPORT AND PLAN	39
THE FIRST TEN YEARS	51
AMOS SHINKLE	59
A NEW SPIRIT	65
BUILDING THE TOWERS	71
BUILDING THE TOWERS: THE SECOND SEASON	83
WORK COMES TO A STOP	92
WAITING	98
WAR	109

	PAGE
SIEGE OF CINCINNATI	116
AT WORK AGAIN	125
BUILDING THE BRIDGE: 1864	135
1865: FIRST YEAR OF PEACE	140
THE FOOT BRIDGE	144
THE BRIDGE COMPLETED	151
OPENING DAY	159
A QUARTER CENTURY OF THE BRIDGE	167
INTO THE TWENTIETH CENTURY	179
THE BRIDGE TODAY	188
DIRECTORS OF THE BRIDGE COMPANY	209

ILLUSTRATIONS

	PAGE
THE BRIDGE TO-DAY	*Frontispiece*
JOHN A. ROEBLING	19
THE FIRST PLAN	41
AMOS SHINKLE, PRESIDENT, 1866–1892	61
THE PONTOON BRIDGE OF 1862	121
WRAPPING THE CABLES	149
THE CABLES COMPLETED	155
THE BRIDGE IN 1867	161
THE OLD BRIDGE: 1880	169
GATEWAY TO THE SOUTH	177
BRADFORD SHINKLE, PRESIDENT, 1892–1909	181
A. CLIFFORD SHINKLE, PRESIDENT, 1909—	185
AERIAL VIEW OF THE FLOOD OF 1937	191
AERIAL VIEW OF THE FLOOD OF 1937—LOOKING EAST	195
COVINGTON IN THE GREAT FLOOD OF 1937	201
TEMPORARY RAMP IN COVINGTON—FLOOD OF 1937	205

THE RIVER

OUT of ages lost in the twilight of the past, out of the oldest mountains in America, the Ohio River gathers its waters. The somber forests of the Appalachians hide the springs from which it flows. Down from the rocky summits, through the deep valleys into the foothills, across the rolling plains and through endless cyprus swamps to the vast prairies of the West, a thousand miles and more the Ohio River flows.

In a past beyond man's reckoning, there was once no Ohio River. The ancient tributaries which come from the mountains on the south and east ran uninterrupted to the north. Ages slipped away, and from the north the massive ice sheet of the Polar Regions began to push out. It spread across Canada and across the basin of the Great Lakes. At last, in central Ohio it came to a stop. The ancient rivers from the south were dammed up. Their waters collected, filling the deep valleys.

A time came when the waters from one flooded valley spilled over and joined those in the next. Thus a great lake was born: Lake Ohio. The waters still poured in from the mountains, and found their way blocked by the ice cap. Seeking an outlet, they finally broke through in the West. Thus was born the Ohio River, gathering water from a quarter of a million square miles, and sending it on to the Mississippi.

In the long years that followed, the Ohio changed its course more than once. One ice age followed another, as the ice cap pushed southward, or retreated toward the Arctic zone. In the neighborhood of Cincinnati, the Ohio River turned northward up the valley of the Little Miami, nearly to Hamilton, Ohio. There it turned again, and flowed south through the Great Miami Valley until it entered its present channel below Cincinnati. The Licking River ran from Kentucky directly across Cincinnati and up Mill Creek Valley. But in time the Ohio found the course that it has today. For thousands of years, it has remained in this channel. Winter snow and summer rain in the mountains have fed it. The dark, green hills have been reflected in its blue-green water. The majesty and color impressed the savage Indian with a deep-felt awe. Few were the villages they built along the Ohio, and rarely did they launch their canoes on its solemn surface.

With the coming of the white man, the Ohio River gained a new importance. It was a mighty highway, carrying men and civilization from the East into the wilderness. But it was also a barrier. The Ohio River was a wall in the path of the wayfarer, a barrier on the road from North to South. Below it lay Dixieland. Above it lay the lands of the great Northwest. Below it, farmers planted cotton and tobacco; above, grew wheat and corn. Two civilizations sprang up, one on either shore, divided and alien. The barrier of water wanted a bridge.

IN NEED OF A BRIDGE

THE first pioneers to the West came across the mountains of Virginia, south of the Ohio River. Blazing trails through the forest, planting corn in the clearings, they began to fill up Kentucky. On the other side of the Ohio, to the north, was Indian country. Bands of painted savages roamed through the wilderness there, and frequently they crossed the river to attack the Kentucky settlements. The Indians, with their light canoes, moved easily. Many times the Kentucky pioneers, still landsmen and unused to river travel, must have wished for some ready way to return the attack. Many times they must have wished to cross the Ohio and put a stop to the Indian menace.

After a few years, pioneers began moving into the land north of the Ohio. From Brownsville and Pittsburgh they floated downstream in flatboats until they came to some pleasant cove. There they would land and establish a farm or settlement. Such a party came in 1788 to the broad plain opposite the mouth of the Licking River. Landing at a little inlet on the Ohio shore, they built the first cabins of Cincinnati.

Between pioneer Cincinnati and the nearest important white settlement up the Ohio lay hundreds of miles of wilderness. Wolves and bears were among the least dangers which the forests held. But across the Ohio River, only eighty miles to the south, was the city of Lexington, Kentucky. It was already one of the oldest and wealthiest cities in this new western country. Cincinnati merchants bought their supplies in Lexington. Farmers in Ohio looked to that city for tools and seed. Many early ministers and lawyers came from the Kentucky Bluegrass to work in the village on the north shore of the Ohio. And during the Indian wars from 1790 to 1815, thousands of Kentucky militiamen crossed the Ohio River at Cincinnati, on their way to battlefields further north. For trade, for travelers, and for defense, ready communication across the Ohio River was a necessity.

Only three years after the first log cabins were built at Cincinnati, Winthrop Sargent, Secretary of the Northwest Territory, authorized the first ferry across the river. In a proclamation of February 13, 1792, he established it "for the public interests and the convenience of the inhabitants of the county of Hamilton." The ferry linked Ohio with Virginia, for Kentucky was then but a county of Virginia. It served for many years, but not always for the convenience of the people. Ice blocked the river; floating timber and debris damaged or sunk the boats; floods swept them away, and the rates of toll were sometimes excessive.

THE OHIO BRIDGE

Meanwhile the little country town of Cincinnati grew steadily larger. When President Jefferson bought Louisiana from the French in 1803, some local businessmen saw a great opportunity. They set up a bank to finance exports to the Far West. But it was too early a day for this to flourish. The boys still looked for stray cattle in the willow bottoms along Mill Creek and in the groves of yellow poplar around the city. They still picked blackberries in a thicket in the heart of town. On the Fourth of July a brass band paraded up and down the dusty streets. In winter, the men sat around the stove in the store, chewing black tobacco and talking about the latest news of Napoleon.

Then in 1811 the first steamboat puffed around a bend in the river, and everybody in Cincinnati marveled at the new invention. The War of 1812 came along, and lanky, leather-clothed volunteers crowded to the recruiting station in the town. They were filled with excitement, and brought excitement with them. A brand new steam cotton mill was put up, the first real factory in the town.

By 1815 Cincinnati developed a fever for great things. "Some enthusiastic persons already speak of a bridge across the Ohio at Cincinnati," wrote Daniel Drake in his *Picture of Cincinnati;* though he cautiously added, "the period at which this great project can be executed is certainly remote." A bridge across the Ohio—across a river a quarter of a mile wide! Nowhere in the world was there such a bridge. These people in the raw frontier were thinking of things the greatest engineers in Europe scarcely dreamed of.

Four more years passed. Across the river, the town of Covington was laid out, and the first houses were built there. The riflemen defeated the Indians in the War of 1812, and the countryside was at last safe. Farmers began to move up into the Miami country to raise wheat and corn. Cincinnati engineers built their first steamboat in 1816. Apples, cheese, pork, and brandy were carted to the many steamboat landings, loaded, and shipped down the river to the new southern markets at Memphis and Vicksburg, Natchez and New Orleans. And people still talked of a bridge.

In the first *Cincinnati Directory*, Oliver Farnsworth wrote about it in 1819: "Some considerable discussion has at various times agitated the public, touching the practicability of bridging the Ohio opposite Cincinnati. Many have ridiculed it as an hypothesis, at once absurd and visionary, whilst others have viewed it in a more serious light. It is now satisfactorily ascertained that a bridge may be permanently constructed, and at an expense vastly inferior to what has generally been supposed. . . . There is little doubt, if we can be allowed to form an opinion from the public enterprise which now distinguishes our inhabitants, that very few years will elapse before a splendid bridge will unite Cincinnati with Newport and Covington."

THE OHIO BRIDGE

Dr. Daniel Drake thought in 1815 that the bridge was "certainly remote"; four years later it appeared within the prospect of "very few years." Great changes had come to Cincinnati in those four years. The bedraggled little town suddenly boomed. The coming of the steamboat brought cheap and fast service for travelers and goods. Thousands of young men, poor in money but rich in ambition, rushed out from the East. An inland empire was springing up before their eyes. It was going to be vaster, more wealthy, and more powerful than any the world had ever seen. No wonder these men had visions of great deeds.

EARLY PLANS AND BRIDGES

BUILDING bridges calls for more than vision. It calls for capital; and capital was scarce in the new country of the West. The first bridge at Cincinnati was a long frail footwalk over Deer Creek, built around 1800.

Two years before, in 1798, a citizens' committee led by Judge Symmes and William Henry Harrison (who was later to be elected ninth President of the United States) was barely able to raise $290 for a bridge across Mill Creek. It was not half enough, and the bridge had to wait for another eight years. Then in the summer of 1806 Mr. Parker built the bridge near the mouth of the stream, using the yellow poplar that grew along the creek.

A year or two later, during a spring freshet, a boat was fastened beneath the bridge. When the water rose, the boat rose and lifted the bridge on its back. Together the boat and bridge drifted off down the Ohio to destruction. With the bridge went Parker's investment of $700.

The next bridge over Mill Creek was built by Ethan Stone in 1811. It, too, was carried off by a flood, in 1822. Stone tried building another bridge across Mill Creek shortly after the flood wrecked his first one. This one stood for ten years, until the great flood of 1832. Then the whole structure floated off and came to rest on an island six miles above Louisville. So precious was the bridge that it was towed all the way back to Cincinnati and reinstalled. It stayed in use for many years thereafter.

A bridge across the Ohio continued to be the subject of discussion for several years. In 1826 it found its way into print once more. Daniel Drake and Edward Mansfield wrote in their book on Cincinnati in that year that the bridge was as practical as it was important. "The scarcity of capital among our citizens may delay it for a few more years," they wrote, "but the period is manifestly not remote when its construction will be undertaken."

"The feasibility of throwing a permanent bridge over the Ohio at this place, at an expense which would secure a handsome interest upon the sum required for its accomplishment, is generally admitted by those practical, calculating men, who have had the subject under consideration, and who have possessed the existing data from which to draw their conclusions."

The plans which were drawn up at this early date for an Ohio River bridge are amusing. It would be sixteen hundred thirty feet long, the estimated distance across the Ohio from the foot of Broadway, Cincinnati. Besides the abutments on each side of the river, the entire structure would be carried on eight or nine piers. In the main section, across the channel of the Ohio, there would be a drawbridge to permit the passage of boats. This section across the channel, a distance of two hundred feet, they thought was not too broad for a single span; but if it were necessary, an intermediate pier could be built there. Finally, this was to be a Y-bridge. It would extend from Broadway, on the Cincinnati side, to some point in the mouth of the Licking. There it would branch, with one arm going to Newport, east of the Licking, and one to Covington, on the west.

Estimates of the cost of this elaborate building ran from $100,000 to $200,000. Surplus capital from the East was looked for to finance the construction; and the expense, it was expected, would be paid for by the usual means of tolls.

Whatever the reason may have been, little was done with the project of a bridge for another ten years. Money was invested heavily in building steamboats and turnpikes, especially the new macadam roads; and it was invested in manufacturing. But it was not available for a bridge.

Half a century had passed since the first pioneers came to Cincinnati. A dozen new States had been carved out of the Western forests. The little cluster of mud-plastered log cabins was a flourishing city with miles of neat red brick homes. Commerce from half the nation crowded its public wharf. The need for a bridge was greater than ever before; yet there was nothing but talk to show for it.

FROM TALK TO ACTION

FOR a quarter of a century men had been talking about an Ohio River bridge. It was time to begin doing something about it. By an odd turn of fortune, the real movement for a bridge did not come either from Covington or Cincinnati. It came from a city eighty miles from the river. It was in Lexington, Kentucky, that the first steps beyond mere discussion were taken to secure a bridge over the Ohio.

The explanation lies in the changing trade routes of the West. In pioneer days, the chief trade through Cincinnati ran along a north-south line. It went up the Miami Rivers to the north, into the "little Corn Belt" of Ohio, and it went up the Licking to the south, to the Kentucky Bluegrass and to Lexington. But after the steamboat was invented, traffic began to change. It now cut directly across its former route. It followed the Ohio River from Pennsylvania in the east, between Ohio and Kentucky, down to the Mississippi. Products of farm and factory, corn and wool, nails and crockery were loaded on the steamboats till they could hold no more, and thus they were shipped down the river, down to the new "Cotton Kingdom" of the South.

During the 1830's proud, aristocratic old Lexington discovered that she was falling far behind in the race for glory. The steamboat had suddenly made the Ohio River the great highway to wealth—and Lexington was not on the river. To overcome the handicap, Lexington depended on roads. For a time the roads helped out. Like spokes from the hub of a wheel they ran from Lexington to three ports on the Ohio: Maysville, Covington, and Louisville. The Covington road was unimproved, and bore little traffic. The Maysville and the Louisville Turnpikes, however, gave Lexington ready access to the river. At the same time these roads aided Lexington business, they helped to develop the river cities to an even greater extent.

To overcome this, Lexington businessmen joined with groups from Cincinnati and from Charleston, South Carolina, to promote a railway. The railway was to go from Cincinnati to the sea. Passing through Lexington, it would restore some of her lost trade.

Suddenly Lexington discovered that her "right and left bowers," as she proudly referred to her river ports of Maysville and Louisville, had become her rivals. They were doing all they could to prevent the building of the railroad. That railroad would cut into their market in central Kentucky too deeply. It would take business away from the river ports by giving direct connections with the sea at Charleston. Louisville and Maysville businessmen thought they could not afford to let the railroad go through. It was never built. Yet Lincoln himself declared in 1861 that the Civil War would not have come if this railroad from Cincinnati to Charleston had been built in the years after 1835.

The people of Lexington and Fayette County, Kentucky, gave up hope of ever finishing their railroad. Then they began "for the first time, seriously to consider the propriety of forming commercial connections with Cincinnati." Early in the spring of 1839 they held a public meeting "with reference to the erection of a bridge across the Ohio River, from Covington to Cincinnati." To carry this out, they proposed a convention in Cincinnati, and elected delegates to go to the Ohio metropolis.

When this news came to Cincinnati, elaborate preparations were made to receive the visitors. Nathan Guilford, a lawyer educated at Yale University, and the father of the Ohio Public School system, gathered a committee to co-operate with the men from Lexington. That meeting, the warm, cloudy Saturday night of March 23, 1839, just one hundred years ago, was the first ever held in Cincinnati looking toward the Ohio Bridge. The group met at the City Council Chambers, where his Honor the mayor, Samuel W. Davies, was called to the chair. After a number of resolutions urging better commercial connections were adopted, plans were made for a public meeting to be held two weeks later. At that meeting, on April 5, the delegates from Lexington would be present.

Meantime, other cities and towns along the

way took up the idea and joined in enthusiastically. The delegates from Lexington stopped along the way to Cincinnati, and picked up others from Georgetown and Covington, Kentucky.

Finally, on Friday evening, April 5, "a highly respectable portion of the citizens" of Cincinnati met in the Hall of the old Cincinnati College to hear the combined delegations. But as their resolutions finally shaped up, a committee of ten was appointed "for the purpose of obtaining subscriptions from the citizens of Cincinnati, for the stock of the Lexington, Georgetown, and Covington Turnpike Company." Though a number of prominent Cincinnati steamboat men, insurance men, and politicians took part in the business, the public response was slight.

The money to improve the road from Covington to Lexington was raised, and the road was improved. Both cities found it to their advantage. But the proposals for a bridge which started this campaign dropped into the background.

The Ohio Bridge seemed more remote than ever before. The plans which were suggested in 1826 were now impossible, for the steamboat traffic had grown so heavy that no such bridge could be built. It would block the movement of the boats to an intolerable extent. Yet no alternative plan for a bridge had been offered. The old need for a bridge remained; it was greater than ever before. But the new problem of a heavy steamboat trade defied solution. There seemed to be no practical way out.

At this very moment, when the high hopes for

a bridge had so speedily been put on the shelf, the path out of this dilemma was being cleared. Two men were working on plans which would revolutionize bridge building. One of them, Charles Ellet, lived in Philadelphia. The other, John Roebling, was even closer by. He lived along the headwaters of the Ohio at Pittsburgh. Those two men were each on the brink of a solution which would make the bridge a possibility.

JOHN A. ROEBLING

JOHN ROEBLING lived in the ancient German city of Muhlhausen. His father was a moderately prosperous tobacco manufacturer. The fragrance of his wares filled the old homestead where the family lived. It blended with the atmosphere of peace and contentment.

Young John had left Muhlhausen and gone to the great Prussian capital, Berlin. There he studied at the Royal Polytechnic Institute. He took courses in architecture, bridge construction, and hydraulics, as well as languages and philosophy. His teachers were the foremost scientists of the age, and the great philosopher Hegel. In due time Roebling received the degree of Civil Engineer, and for three years after that he worked for the Prussian government, building roads and bridges.

The government work was always the same, always rigidly prescribed, according to the same old rules. The everlasting red tape would allow no experimentation, no improvements. There was no future in it for a man with ambition.

Roebling was a young man with ideas of his own. He wanted to be a great bridge builder.

He had gone to the old cathedral town of Bamberg, Bavaria; and there he had studied a remarkable chain suspension bridge. The idea of suspending a bridge was good; but Roebling thought they did not yet know the right way to do it. He had other ideas, and he wanted to try them out. He thought that if he had the chance, he could build better bridges than anyone before him.

In Germany, Roebling wrote, things could be done only with "an army of councillors, ministers, and other officials, discussing the matter for ten years, making long journeys, and writing long reports, while the money spent in all these preliminaries comes to more than the actual accomplishment of the enterprise."

Young Roebling was at home in Muhlhausen, back from his work, in the winter of 1829-1830. He was talking with his elder brother Karl. They were not talking of plans for bridges. They were not even talking about the stodgy, poky ways of their Fatherland. There was something else passing between them, something that was in the air in Muhlhausen, and all over the Old World.

Family acquaintances had just come back for a visit from America. Among them was an engineer named Etzler, a close friend of Roebling's. Etzler told the two young men of the opportunities in the New World. There, in America, a man was on his own. He was not tied down by tradition and century-old conservatism. Etzler suggested making up a party in

John A. Roebling

Muhlhausen to move to America and set up a little colony of their own.

Karl and John liked the idea. They would be among friends; they would live in a democratic country, where they could govern themselves; and they would be free from the narrow prejudices and harsh restrictions of the little German tyrants. It was an attractive proposition to the two young men. Talking about it, they gazed out of the window onto the broad street that led to Erfurt, and beyond that to Leipzig and Berlin, and on to the sea.

Yet John Roebling could not make up his mind to go. There was change in the air; change that might alter the course of history; change that might make it possible for a man to get ahead in the world, even in Saxony and Prussia. Winter melted into spring, and spring warmed into summer.

Suddenly, in midsummer, at the end of July, 1830, word came of revolution in France. The old Bourbon tyranny was finally overthrown! In three wild days, with paving stones, trees, barrels, boxes, and carts piled in the streets for barricades, the citizens of Paris drove out the king's troops, dethroned Charles X, and called in a new, liberal monarch, Louis Philippe.

The news spread into Germany like fire. Hopes mounted high; and young Roebling may have looked for an explosion at home that would shake off the old official inertia. He understood that inertia well. His own father was one of the placid, well-to-do burghers in his home town. But the revolution passed through Germany with a tremor like a distant earthquake. A few reforms were made, in Hesse-Cassel, in Saxony, in Hanover, and in Brunswick. The great states of Prussia and Austria were unmoved.

Once again the Roeblings thought of leaving the old country. John and his brother wrote to a friend in Hamburg about coming to America. What information could he give them? Their friend replied in mid-August; and then, suddenly, a week later, news flashed in of another revolution. A new nation was born, Belgium. It was created in the last days of August and September as an independent country, released from foreign rule. Liberalism seemed once again on the way. Perhaps it would yet be unnecessary to leave for America.

Then just as suddenly repression bore down in full force. It was illegal for a skilled workman to leave the country, and Roebling's friend from America, Etzler, was thrown in jail for suggesting migration to the New World. The rest of the men involved in the plan found their actions closely watched by spies. Their mail was censored by the police. If oppression had been burdensome before, it now became intolerable. During the fall and winter of 1830-1831 John Roebling and his friends definitely agreed to leave for America. But they had to move with the greatest caution and secrecy. One false step and they might all be arrested. John Roebling was already notorious as one of the half-dozen most ardent liberals of Muhlhausen.

At length all their plans were complete. On May 11, 1831, the two Roebling brothers left Muhlhausen for the great seaport of Bremen. There they chartered a small boat, the *August Eduard,* to take them and their friends across the Atlantic. On May 23 they left, by way of England, for America. Heavy winds drove them far from their course. They were threatened by pirates. After eleven weeks at sea, on August 6 they reached Philadelphia.

In Philadelphia, Roebling lived for a time in a boarding-house, practicing his English and looking around for a good location for his colony. He decided against settling in the South because of slavery. The Far West was too far away, and called for too much capital expense. Eventually a place in Butler County, Pennsylvania, about twenty-five miles from Pittsburgh, was chosen. There Roebling and his friends bought seven thousand acres of farm land. In two years they had a flourishing little village, first named Germania, and later Saxonburg.

John Roebling was trained to be an engineer, not a farmer. He read many books on farming; but he was impatient of that unscientific thing, the weather. At first he found an outlet for his energies in building roads and houses, digging cellars and wells. But as a farmer, he was not a success.

In 1837 Roebling had a chance to return to his

true vocation. Pennsylvania needed a State engineer to supervise the design and construction of dams and locks on the newly planned State canals. Roebling offered his services, and was appointed in the same year that he became an American citizen.

The next few years of Roebling's life were filled with various activities in engineering. First he worked on the Sandy and Beaver Canal, then on a feeder of the Pennsylvania Canal, along the Allegheny River, and finally on the strange combination of canal, highway, and railroad over the Allegheny Mountains, by which Philadelphia hoped to outmatch New York in commerce.

While busy at this work, on January 28, 1840, Roebling wrote offering his services to Charles Ellet, a well-known civil engineer and bridge builder. Ellet was at that time planning bridges over the Schuylkill River at Philadelphia and over the Mississippi at St. Louis.

"The study of suspension bridges," Roebling wrote, "formed for the last few years of my residence in Europe my favorite occupation; as this matter, however, appeared to be little cared for by engineers in this country, I had no occasion whatever to bestow any further attention on it, while engaged in professional pursuits here."

"Some publications of yours, which appeared in the R. R. Journal on the subject of suspension bridges, revived in me the old favorite ideas, and I was agreeably surprised by the report of your being now actually engaged in making preparations for constructing a wire cable bridge over the Schuylkill at Pha. and another over the Mississippi at St. Louis, which latter indeed would form the greatest construction of the kind in existence. . . .

"Let but a single bridge of the kind be put up in Pha. exhibiting all the beautiful forms of the system to the best advantage, and it needs no prophecy to foretell the effect, which the novel and useful features will produce upon the intelligent minds of the Americans."

CHARLES ELLET

CHARLES ELLET, the man to whom Roebling addressed his letter, was the foremost bridge builder in America. The son of a Pennsylvania farmer, Ellet left the home of his eccentric father at seventeen to work as a rodman on a railway survey. Within a short time he rose to be an assistant engineer. Then, feeling the need of more formal education, in 1830 he went to study at the Ecole Polytechnique in Paris. There he was an eyewitness of the revolution which inspired Roebling in that year. After returning to America, Ellet worked at civil engineering; and in 1834 he proposed building a suspension bridge over the Potomac.

The year after Ellet received Roebling's letter (which apparently went unanswered), he built the first important suspension bridge in America. Completed in 1842 at a cost of $35,000, this bridge crossed the Schuylkill River at Fairmount, near Philadelphia.

Ellet proceeded quickly from one work to another. As his bridges sprang up, his ambitions continued to spread. Before long he was talking of building a bridge across the Ohio. In a pamphlet which he published, Ellet suggested that a bridge would be possible at several points along the river. He named Madison, Indiana; Louisville and Maysville, Kentucky; Marietta, Ohio, and Wheeling, Virginia, as places where a bridge could be built without a single pier in the water. There were many other places, he added, where it could be built with but one pier.

Ellet emphasized the need for keeping the channel of the river unobstructed; and he wrote at length of the beauty, safety, strength, and utility of suspension bridges. He suggested that an Ohio bridge should have a height of eighty feet above the "summer surface" of the water, because of the many freshets which caused quick rises in the river. Thus curiously the first engineer's proposal for a suspension bridge over the Ohio River came from Philadelphia. The proposal was not lost on local businessmen.

With the idea of suspension bridges in the air, Cincinnati constructors soon had to try it out. The first local example was built in 1843, the very year after the Schuylkill bridge was completed. It was a little bridge, only sixty feet long, across the Miami Canal at Race Street; and it was completed in four months at a cost of only $1,650. But it was the first wire suspension bridge west of the mountains.

The idea was next taken up the following summer. In June, 1844, a bridge between Covington and Newport, Kentucky, across the Licking River, was proposed. A charter for such a bridge had been issued in 1830, but nothing had yet been accomplished. Besides the obvious advantages of a bridge between the sister cities of northern Kentucky, there was now a new angle to this. "This demonstration," an anonymous promoter wrote about the proposed Covington and Newport bridge, "will doubtless be followed at a distant day by one still more *emphatic,* which shall unite for all future time the city of *Cincinnati* with her younger, smaller, but not less worthy sister of Kentucky, and that, too, by a *bridge across the Ohio River.*"

A month later, at the end of July, 1844, a correspondent of the *Licking Valley Register* presented a long argument for the Covington and Newport bridge. He climaxed it with this final reason, "It is the sure entering wedge to a much greater enterprise, viz., a bridge across the Ohio, at Cincinnati."

By the close of another year the movement had gone so far that Colonel Long, of Kentucky, declared the Ohio River bridge could be built for $150,000, "and the architect of the wire bridge, now in course of erection over the Allegheny River, at Pittsburgh, himself a deserved celebrity as a builder of bridges, we understand is willing to construct it for $100,000.

The anonymous master bridge builder, the "deserved celebrity" to whom Colonel Long referred, was John Roebling.

THE COVINGTON AND CINCINNATI BRIDGE COMPANY

THE Ohio River bridge was no longer just a romantic scheme. It was a practical matter so far as engineering was concerned. Bridge builders had discovered how to suspend the long span across the river. Charles Ellet had suggested building a suspension bridge across the Ohio; and John Roebling had volunteered to do it.

The old obstacle still remained the chief handicap: there was not enough capital. It was even worse in the early 1840's than before. The eastern part of the country had been struck by a financial panic in 1837, and this reached the West in 1839. The depression which followed grew worse year by year. Shops and factories shut down; banks failed; new businesses sprang up, only to be driven to the wall in a few months. From 1841 to 1843 Cincinnati, along with New York and Philadelphia, had to organize emergency relief committees. Thousands of unemployed were supplied with fuel and clothing, bean soup and bread.

After seven such lean years, in 1845 the country seemed to turn a corner. A slogan was invented, America's *Manifest Destiny*. Everyone began to talk about it. Nobody quite knew what it meant, but it sounded good. The great Republic of Texas was added to the United States in March, 1845; and in the fall negotiations were started with Great Britain to get Oregon for the Union. That would give the Republic a seacoast and a port on the Pacific. America would spread from sea to sea! The future held promise of great things. It was America's *Manifest Destiny* to become the greatest nation on earth.

With a brighter outlook, businessmen began to talk more optimistically of their plans. All through the country, and especially in the South, they arranged commercial conventions. The people of northern Kentucky, like those elsewhere, felt that the country was at last on the upgrade. During the summer of 1845 talk went around of a local commercial convention. Local newspapers up and down the Licking River mentioned the idea. From the idea would come a plan, which was to include plans for an Ohio River bridge; and from the convention, the Covington and Cincinnati Bridge Company was to be formed.

But once again, it was not the people of Cincinnati nor of Covington who took the first steps. The first move was made in a little town forty miles up the Licking.

One bright afternoon, the first Saturday in October, the farmers and merchants of Pendleton County, Kentucky, were gathered as usual around the court house in Falmouth. They had shared in the talk of a convention. They were interested especially in the improvement of the Licking River so that boats could travel easily down to the Ohio, and goods be brought up from Covington at low cost. That Saturday they elected delegates to go to Covington, to see what could be done about it. If it were possible, they were going to hold a general Licking Navigation Convention.

The idea was popular, and the next Saturday a meeting was scheduled for Covington; but it was called off because the weather was bad. A week later, however, the people of Kenton County met at Independence, Kentucky, and elected delegates, among whom were J. W. Menzies and Robert Wallace. In the meantime, other towns along the Licking River held town meetings and elected delegates to go to Covington for a convention.

On the last Thursday in October, 1845, the convention met in Covington. Three major questions were put before it. One of them was the improvement of navigation in the Licking. A second one was the old project calling for an extension of the Charleston, South Carolina, and Cincinnati Railroad, of which only a small part had been finished.

The third was introduced by the resolution of Robert Wallace, though it was surely in the mind of every delegate present. It called for "a bridge across the Ohio, at Covington."

From this time on, the idea of an Ohio bridge

was not allowed to drop, even for a week. Colonel Long, who had first suggested Roebling as an architect, declared the bridge could be built for $150,000. The stock for such a bridge would all be subscribed in a single month. People would *scramble* for it.

By the end of the year a group of men were planning to get a charter for the bridge. The mayor of Covington called a citizens' meeting on Monday night, December 8, at his office, "for the purpose of taking steps to obtain a charter for a bridge over the Ohio at this place."

"We see no good reason," the mayor announced, "why the application for a charter should be rejected. The public interest requires the erection of a bridge, and we do not believe that either the Kentucky or Ohio Legislature will take the responsibility of preventing the execution of this great work. No time is to be lost, and by acting with energy our object may easily be secured."

When the meeting convened, John K. McNickle was called to the chair, and John S. Finley was appointed secretary. Henry B. Brown, editor of the *Licking Valley Register*, offered a series of five resolutions. The first resolved "That in the opinion of this meeting, it is highly important to the interests of this city and to the interests of the public at large, that a bridge should be constructed as soon as practicable over the Ohio River between Covington and Cincinnati."

The other resolutions stated that such a bridge

would not injure navigation on the Ohio, or injure the interests or rights of any individual; that committees should be appointed to visit the State Legislatures of Ohio and Kentucky; and to obtain signatures in Kentucky for a petition to the Legislature for the charter; and to wait on the people of Cincinnati in an endeavor to induce them to unite with the Covington men in promoting the objects of this meeting. Finally, it was resolved to publish the proceedings of the meeting in Covington and Cincinnati newspapers.

The first committee appointed at the mayor's meeting in Covington named five men to visit the State Legislatures of Ohio and Kentucky. They were John S. Finley and Charles A. Withers, Covington councilmen; H. J. Groesbeck and J. W. Menzies; and Henry B. Brown, the editor of the *Licking Valley Register*.

The second committee, appointed to secure signatures to petitions, included ten men. Among them were three Covington councilmen, F. Riggs, C. A. Withers, and Fred G. Gedge; and W. E. Ashbrook, L. F. Daugherty, T. Timberlake, Harvey Lewis, J. B. Casey, W. R. Thomas, and William Brown.

The Kentucky General Assembly met in Frankfort a few days later, and soon the Covington lobbyists were on hand. On February 17, 1846, the long-sought charter was at last enacted. By its terms, six Cincinnatians and nine Covingtonians, a group of fifteen men "with their associates be and hereby are created a body politic and corporate, by the name of the Covington and Cincinnati Bridge Company."

The names of these men, some of which had not appeared before, were James Goodloe, George Carlisle, E. Foote, Robert Buchanan, Thomas M. Minor, and William S. Johnson, all of Cincinnati; and from Covington, James G. Arnold, John S. Finley, John B. Casey, Charles A. Withers, Herman J. Groesbeck, Frederick G. Gedge, John K. McNickle, George M. Southgate, and Mortimer M. Benton.

Thus the company was created and launched in a world of many troubles.

THE FIRST ROUND

SHORTLY before the charter was issued to the Bridge Company by the Kentucky Legislature, some of the men in the group wrote to Roebling to ask about a bridge plan. At the time Roebling was busy with the last-minute work on the new Monongahela Suspension Bridge, which was nearly completed at Pittsburgh. On the same day that this bridge was opened for wagon traffic, January 31, 1846, Roebling answered the questions from Cincinnati.

In the letter which he wrote, Roebling outlined briefly his ideas on the subject. His plan called for a single arch of twelve hundred feet. At either end of the bridge abutments would rise about fifty or sixty feet above the river. This, added to an ascent of forty feet, would give the bridge a height of ninety or one hundred feet above the river. Such an elevation, Roebling believed, would permit steamboats to clear even at a high stage of water.

In the same letter, Roebling offered an alternative plan which could be constructed at less expense. It called for two piers in the river. These would support a center span of six hundred to seven hundred feet across the channed. Two spans of lesser dimensions would connect at each end with the shore. "But I for one," wrote

Roebling, "would say, do not obstruct 'La belle riviere'—there is but one in the world."

Either of these plans would be permitted under the terms of the charter which was then before the Kentucky Legislature. No restrictions were placed either on the length of the span or its height above the river; and the question of using piers in the river was left to the judgment of the company. The only requirement—and it was a very broad one—was "That nothing contained in this act shall be so construed as to authorize the said company to construct any bridge which may obstruct the free and common navigation of the said river Ohio."

Opponents of the bridge became alarmed when they saw how popular it was becoming. Steamboat men, commission merchants, boiler and engine manufacturers, insurance agents, and many others joined forces to oppose it. For more than a month a violent controversy raged. Anti-bridge interests denounced the plan on every ground they could discover. Advocates of the bridge argued that at least wholesale condemnation of the scheme might wait until the details were made public.

The contest was a critical one. The Bridge Company had succeeded in only two months in organizing and getting a charter from Kentucky. Now they were trying to secure permission from the State of Ohio. If they succeeded, work might start on the bridge almost at once. But if anti-bridge interests won out, no one could tell how long a struggle might lie in the future. While the charter was before the Ohio Legislature the fight went on, and no one could see the outcome.

The bridge could not be built, some maintained, without piers in the river. Was there anywhere in the world a bridge that long without piers? No. So obviously, they said, it was impossible to build one. But if the bridge were built, and piers were placed in the river, water would be dammed up. The public landing would be flooded. The city would be ruined. Thus the argument ran.

A bridge to Kentucky would carry business from Ohio to Kentucky, others maintained. Commercial and manufacturing houses would rush across the river. Property values in Cincinnati would be destroyed, they warned; and Cincinnati would become a deserted city.

Still others objected that if the floor of the bridge were only ninety feet above low water, steamboats could not pass under it in safety. Since the whole trade and prosperity of Cincinnati depended on steamboating, the bridge would bring disaster to her business.

A petition was drawn up to oppose the granting of a charter to the Bridge Company in Ohio. But the people of Cincinnati would not sign; and its sponsors hurriedly withdrew it from circulation.

A Cincinnati publicity agent, Charles Cist, announced that he had to correct Roebling on one important matter. If a suspension bridge could be constructed without piers, Cist said, he would "have no hesitation in expressing a favorable opinion upon the project." But, said Cist, the river was not sixteen hundred feet wide, as Roebling had estimated. It was twenty-four hundred feet across. Although Cist tremendously exaggerated the width of the river, in order to make it seem impossible to span it without piers in the water, many people trusted his accuracy. Thus another large group were persuaded that the bridge could not be built without interrupting river traffic.

Finally, there were those who objected to chartering a foreign corporation in Ohio. One man, at least, suspected in the plan a scheme on the part of Kentucky to encroach on the sovereignty of Ohio.

Meanwhile the Ohio Legislature was considering the question. On February 19, 1846, the Senate Committee on Federal Relations submitted its brief report on the bridge. There were only two points in the statement which Mr. Kelley, chairman of the committee, offered to the State Senate: The bridge would depreciate the value of real property in Cincinnati; and it would obstruct the navigation of the Ohio.

The opposition had won out. All those who felt their business depended on defeating the bridge bill celebrated a day of victory, for the State of Ohio refused to charter the company. The first round went against the bridge.

ROEBLING'S REPORT AND PLAN

THE Bridge Company was by no means discouraged at this first set-back. Three months later, in May, 1846, they had Roebling himself in Cincinnati. It was the first time he had ever come here. Roebling, with the aid of another engineer, R. H. Rickey, surveyed the river from Cincinnati to Covington, on the Main Street-Garrard Street line. He measured the banks, and examined the geological structure of the river bed. Having completed his notes, he returned to Pittsburgh.

Four months later Roebling finished his plan. The report which he drew up, dated September 1, was published in Cincinnati immediately with the title, *Report and Plan for a Suspension Bridge, Proposed to be Erected over the Ohio River at Cincinnati*. The 36-page pamphlet contained sections and elevations of the bridge, an elaborate technical discussion, and a brief but brilliant analysis of the commercial problems involved. The "General Remarks," which occupy the first four or five pages of the pamphlet, show a breadth of understanding such as few technically trained engineers then possessed.

Roebling began his argument with an answer

to his critics. Those who oppose the building of a bridge, he said, have repeatedly and unqualifiedly denied the right of States bordering the Ohio River to grant charters for building bridges across that river. They rest their arguments on the ground that the free and uninterrupted navigation of the river is a national object, paramount to any individual or State interest. This, as a general proposition, Roebling admitted was quite correct.

"On the other hand," Roebling pointed out, "it appears but justice that the States should be allowed the right of forming communications across the river, accessible at all seasons, for the promotion of commerce and intercourse, provided such communications do not impede the navigation.

"The idea of bridging the large rivers of the West," he continued, "could not be entertained before the system of suspension bridges was fairly introduced. An attempt at this mode of building in the United States was made about forty years ago, when a number of chain bridges were erected upon a rude and insufficient plan. Although these attempts failed, they clearly demonstrated the practicability of the system. That no further efforts were made to perfect the plan, was not so much owing to the difficulty of construction, as to the great abundance of good timber in most parts of the country, which greatly facilitated the construction of wooden bridges, and reduced their first cost."

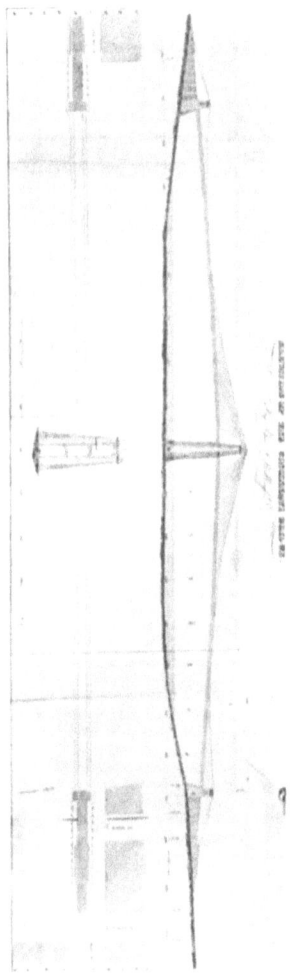

THE FIRST PLAN
Drawn by Roebling. Taken from his *Report and Plan* showing the great central tower in the river

Roebling then proceeded to a discussion of the great bridges which were then being built in Europe. Telford's suspension bridge across the Menai Strait, from the mainland of Wales to the Island of Anglesey, boasted a principal span five hundred and sixty feet in length. The Chester and Holyhead Railway Bridge, in process of construction across the same strait, had two middle spans of four hundred and fifty feet each.

It would appear that spans four hundred feet in length, Roebling decided, would be ample for all purposes of navigation. "But," he proceeded, "there is no necessity of adopting this limit on the Ohio River. The construction of suspension bridges is now so well understood, that no competent builder will hesitate to resort to spans of fifteen hundred feet and more, where localities may require it, and where the object will justify the expense. It may be observed here that, as a general rule, the expense of a superstructure will be in proportion to its span. Large spans will therefore not be adopted without necessity. There are locations, however, where a large span alone is practicable, as where expense can be saved by their adoption, in consequence of the reduction of masonry. The largest suspension bridge in the world, with spans of one thousand feet, is now being erected over the *Danube,* at *Pesth* and *Ofen,* in Hungary, at an elevation sufficient to leave the navigation unobstructed. But it is on the great rivers of the *new world,* where this system of bridge building will, in course of time, be fully applied and perfected."

The next thing Roebling considered was the height of the bridge. The floor of the bridge should be suspended at a height great enough, not only to be above the reach of the highest flood, but to leave navigation unimpeded as well. It was the fear that the bridges would not be high enough to permit the free passage of steamers, which caused most of the opposition to building such bridges across the Ohio.

Roebling announced that he should not countenance a scheme which would be fatal to navigation. But he proposed to explain the situation in such detail that it would end the fears of all those who honestly believed a bridge would mean disaster. He had heard the commander of a steamer say he would consider any bridge an obstruction, even if it were two hundred feet high. "Such objections," Roebling admitted, "are, of course, beyond the reach of argument, and not deserving of any notice."

For the more reasonable objectors, Roebling collected a great mass of evidence. The largest packet on the Ohio River, between Pittsburgh and Cincinnati, was the *Clipper No. 2*. It measured sixty-four feet above water when it was light. The largest boat on the Cincinnati-Louisville run was the *Pike No. 7*, whose chimneys rose sixty-nine feet above the water line. The floor of the proposed bridge would be ninety feet above low water near the wharf, and one hundred and twenty-one feet near the center pier. Thus there was not the shadow of a threat of danger to the boats passing under the bridge.

This defense on the bridge Roebling followed up with a vigorous offensive on the boats. The difficulty came from the height of the steamboat chimney. The higher the chimney, the greater the draft in the furnace; and the greater the draft, the more rapid the combustion of fuel. That, in turn, meant greater speed; and speed was the goal of every steamboat captain. But this, as Roebling next pointed out, was highly wasteful of fuel. It was especially a poor system since there were other more scientific ways of increasing speed.

"High chimneys are the strongest proofs of defective arrangements," he wrote; "they will disappear from our rivers-sooner or later, as improvements advance. They are objectionable in every respect; if they could be forced from our rivers by some low bridge, it would be the greatest service which would be rendered to the navigation of our western waters.

"The ostensible object of high chimneys on board of steamers is, to create more draft. Now, it is fully established and generally known, that economy in fuel is inversely as the rapidity of combustion. And, on the other hand, the escape of lost heat and unconsumed fuel up the chimneys, is in direct proportion to the draft. These, and a few more points, are already better understood on our eastern waters, and in ocean navigation, where economy of fuel is a greater desideratum than here in the West. Chimneys on eastern boats are much lower than on western boats; they are still lower on ocean steamers, where high stacks are very objectionable. The question of an increased speed is there not solved by simply raising the chimneys and increasing the draft, but by other means, a little more creditable to science."

Roebling apologized for having written at greater length on chimneys than he intended; but it was necessary, he explained, to meet the objections which were constantly raised on this matter. He maintained that in the future the power and value of a boat would be estimated not by the height of the chimneys, but by their lowness. *"Low chimneys on a powerful boat,"* he declared, *"will be the best proof of a superior arrangement for the generation of steam."* As there were a number of boats with high chimneys still running, however, and as the fashion seemed likely to continue, he said, "We shall be obliged to adopt in the construction of the proposed work an elevation unnecessarily high." He assumed one hundred and twenty-one feet at the center pier as the maximum to which he could consent.

As an additional comment upon chimneys, Roebling added that there was an easy method of raising and lowering them which was practiced on most ocean steamers. It deserved to be known and applied on the western waters. "Apart from the passage of bridges, or waste of fuel," Roebling concluded, "high chimneys prove objectionable in other respects. They increase the surface exposed to head-winds, make the boat top-heavy, and are in danger of being knocked off, or becoming entangled among the branches of trees, when the boat is running near a shore."

Having turned his sense of humor to good account in these "General Remarks," Roebling passed on to a discussion of the location of the bridge. On his trip to Cincinnati in May, he and Rickey had surveyed the line from Main Street, Cincinnati, to Garrard Street, Covington. It was calculated to be one thousand, six hundred and fifty-eight feet in length. Although the line of Main Street appeared to have some advantages, Roebling observed that it had not been definitely chosen for the location. A bridge was practicable at any point of the city, he said, and concluded, "The general wants of the community will have to be duly considered in the choice of a site, taking into consideration the degree of facility of construction offered by the different locations."

As the charter granted by the Kentucky Legislature left the location of the bridge entirely at the option of the company, Roebling desired that the same provision should be included in the charter to be obtained from the Legislature of Ohio. "It will be to the interest of the company to select the best location," he said, "and as their interests and those of the community are identical, the public will be best served if the company is left entirely free in its choice. Where the business of the community can be best promoted—wherever the greatest intercourse is likely to be, and where the approaches of the bridge do the least injury and offer the greatest accommodations—there will be the most advantageous site."

Finally, before plunging into the technical features of the plan, Roebling sketched a general description of the bridge. "The plan of the bridge, as has been remarked before, is adapted to the profile of the river bed, in line with Main Street: the dimensions, therefore, have reference to that locality. The center line, or axis of the bridge, is supposed to be located at a distance of fifty-five feet from the lower side of Main Street. An open street, as a continuation of Main, would, therefore, be left between the lower return wall of the abutment and the houses now fronting the wharf, of seventy-five feet wide. The length of the bridge, from center to center of the abutments, is fifteen hundred and seventy-six feet; total length, including approaches, two thousand and seventy feet. Two spans are proposed, which will meet in the center of the river upon a gigantic stone pier, of two hundred feet high. Three fourths of the whole suspended weight of the bridge will be supported by this pier.

"The river front of the Cincinnati abutment will be opposite the corner of Wharf and Main" (Wharf Street was a street lying between Water Street and the river, and parallel to both of them) "and nearly in line with Wharf Street.

THE OHIO BRIDGE

It will, therefore, not present any impediment to the current of the river when high. The houses fronting the bridge will be protected by the return walls against the current. These walls extend from the abutment to Front Street, leaving the latter entirely free. The length of the abutment is fifty feet, the extreme width across the return walls, opposite Water Street, will be forty-four feet, and reduced to thirty-eight feet at Front Street. There will, therefore, be a space occupied on the public landing of two hundred and ninety feet long by forty-four feet wide, leaving the wharf between the abutment and the edge of the river entirely free and open. The approach on the Covington side is very nearly the same as on the Cincinnati side. The uniformity and symmetry of the two ends will add much to the splendid appearance which this great structure will present to the eye of the traveler who approaches the city by river."

The tower in the center of the river would, of course, be the most conspicuous part of the whole bridge. From foundation to top it was to measure two hundred feet, rising one hundred and ninety-four feet above low-water mark. Its width was proportioned to the height. It was in reality two towers, each fifteen by forty-three feet at the base and twelve by twenty feet on top. From center to center they would stand forty-five feet apart, in the direction of the river. This would leave space for a roadway about thirty feet wide to pass between them. The two massive walls were to be connected on the foundation and by two arches above. In order to increase the stability, they would be strengthened by buttresses fifteen feet wide at the bottom, seven feet at top, battered fourteen feet. The cubic contents of this pile would be twelve thousand perches, or three hundred thousand cubic feet.

This marvelous structure could be built, Roebling estimated, in three years. Two years would be required to complete the masonry, and the third for the superstructure. It would cost about $375,000—a sum considerably larger than the capital stock of the company provided for. But, once completed, it would last for centuries to come.

THE FIRST TEN YEARS

OPPONENTS of the bridge lost no time once Roebling's report was issued. They saw that the Bridge Company was proceeding in all earnestness, even though the charter had been defeated in the Ohio Legislature. Early in 1847 they published an anonymous pamphlet under the title, *Remarks Upon Mr. Roebling's "Plan and Report for a Wire Suspension Bridge, Proposed to be Erected Over the Ohio River, at Cincinnati."*

The eighteen-page essay contained a strongly worded argument against the bridge. It was supported by plans and calculations made by the Cincinnati City Surveyor, the Hamilton County Surveyor, James Cooper, and Captain Joseph Pierce, an insurance agent who had been for eleven years Port Warden of Cincinnati.

Roebling's witticisms failed to slay the critics of the bridge, who remarked that modern science might all be very well in the East; but in the West they would do as they pleased about chimneys and boilers.

The arguments presented were eight in all. Bridge piers would deflect water from the channel toward the shores. They would increase the height of floods, and increase the speed of the river so that flatboats and other small craft would be unable to land at the wharf below the bridge. The obstruction of the center pier would form a nucleus around which a shoal, bar, or island would form. Boats would too easily be grounded, wrecked, or sunk against towers or piers in the water. Masses of floating ice would destroy the pier and cause the bridge to collapse in the water. The chances of wreck would send up the premium of insurance to rates that would seriously interfere with the profitability of business. The pier would directly interrupt the passage of boats, by compelling them to leave the channel; and finally, the pier and abutments, by damming up the water in the river, would have the effect of creating a permanent flood. It was a terrible picture which these critics drew of the future.

"And if it be said that these dangers are problematical," wrote the anonymous authors, "so we say, are all the advantages promised from it. But be it ever remembered, that for obtaining these advantages, we have other ways, but that for these evils there will be no cure. Let us look, therefore, before we make this leap in the dark, for, the step once made, it can never be recalled."

By way of conclusion, the opponents of the bridge observed that the wisdom of the Legislature in deferring action upon the project the winter before was fully justified by Mr. Roebling's own "Report and Plan." Roebling, they announced, had conceded, virtually, that the plan of a single span was visionary and impossible. The new plan of a center pier for the bridge had still to come before the Legislature. They trusted that it would act with equal wisdom on this new proposal. It would be a mistake to leave these matters to the incorporators or stockholders. The notion that the Legislature was bound to give them a charter and leave the risks and results upon their shoulders was false.

"Posterity will find no satisfaction, and but little justification in this," they warned, "for the accumulation of injury which it is submitted must result to Cincinnati, to Ohio, to the Union, from any such work as is now proposed."

The new attack was effective. The State Legislature met in Columbus, but it passed no charter for the Bridge Company. The Mexican War began, and the young men of Covington and Cincinnati marched gaily off to fight with Old Rough and Ready. General Scott took Vera Cruz, and the war came to an end. But still there was no charter for the Bridge Company.

Up the Ohio River, at Wheeling, Virginia, another bridge company was more successful. It had secured a charter, and Charles Ellet was at work there on the largest bridge he had yet tried to build. In January, 1849, while he was in Wheeling, Ellet published a sixteen-page *Letter* to the Bridge Company at Cincinnati. The letter was written at the request of eight men, R. Buchanan, Dr. John Locke, Henry E. Spencer, and William S. Johnson, of Cincinnati; and Charles A. Withers, John B. Casey, P. S. Bush, and M. M. Benton, of Covington.

Ellet proposed to build a suspension bridge from Cincinnati to Covington with a single arch of fourteen hundred feet. It would be one hundred and twelve feet above low water, or fifty feet above the level of the flood of 1832. Some boats, Ellet admitted, had stacks more than fifty feet in height; but, he said, such boats had no business out in a sixty-foot flood. The cost of this bridge Ellet estimated at $300,000, thus meeting all the terms of the Bridge Company. In conclusion he wrote an eloquent prophecy of the bridge:

"Spanning the Ohio like a rainbow, it cannot fail to become an object of admiration to the country, a most striking monument to the enterprise of the day, and a worthy ornament to your beautiful and flourishing cities."

The *Letter* was published at Columbus on January 15, 1849. With this plan and with the example of a bridge almost finished at Wheeling, the Ohio Legislature changed its mind. More than three years after Kentucky chartered the Bridge Company, Ohio at last took favorable action. On March 26, 1849, the Legislature passed an act declaring that the Covington and Cincinnati Bridge Company, created by act of the State of Kentucky, on February 17, 1846, "Shall be and the same is hereby made a body corporate and politic of this State, with the same franchises, rights, and privileges, and subject to the same duties and liabilities as are specified in the above recited act. . . ."

But the Ohio Legislature made seven exceptions to the charter. The first two of these were especially important for the construction of the bridge. First, "That the said company shall not erect any bridge over the Ohio River, in the erection or continuation whereof a pier or piers may be requisite." Second, "That the said bridge shall not be of less span than fourteen hundred feet, nor of less elevation at the center of the river, than one hundred and twelve feet above low water mark."

Acceptance of this charter by the Bridge Company was received by the Ohio Secretary of State about eight months later, on December 7, 1849. Four of the first ten years of the Bridge Company's existence had thus gone by.

Yet even these limitations were not enough to satisfy the opponents of the bridge. In the spring of 1850, only four months later, the first amendment was passed to the charter. It restricted the location of the bridge. When the city of Covington had been planned in 1815, the streets were so laid out as to lie directly opposite the main streets of Cincinnati. Indeed, but for the interruption of the river, they appeared to be continuations of the same streets. It was the hope of the bridge sponsors that the bridge might form the last link in one of these lines of communication.

On March 26/28, 1850, the act was passed which provided for the terminus of the bridge in Cincinnati. It had to lie between the river and Front Street, and between Walnut Street and "Western Row" (Central Avenue). This much the planners of the bridge might readily agree to. But the amendment further provided that the bridge should enter no "lands now used for public travel upon Vine, Race, Elm, and Plum Streets."

Thus at one stroke the Bridge Company was forbidden to build directly in the line of any of the Cincinnati streets, each of which ran down to the river front. Years later, when the bridge was opened, Roebling observed that everyone, even those who had put this amendment through, regretted the shortsightedness of the move. It deprived Cincinnati forever of one of "the finest and most magnificent avenues on this continent. No avenue in any of the large capitals of Europe," Roebling noted, "could now compare in beauty of grandeur with that long vista which would be presented by the line of Vine Street on the one side, continued in a straight course by Scott Street on the opposite shore, and connected across the river through the imposing arches of the great towers of the suspension bridge."

A short time later another disaster overtook the Bridge Company. At the commencement of the agitation for a suspension bridge, many enthusiasts had recommended a structure connecting Newport with Covington. Many of those who endorsed it did so with the hope that, when its success was demonstrated, the Covington and Cincinnati bridge would find readier approval.

After many delays and false starts, the Licking River Suspension Bridge, from Covington to Newport, was at last completed. In 1853 it was opened. The cost was $80,000, but the value of the bridge seemed likely to exceed even that large expense. For two weeks after it was opened, all went well. Then one day, while a drove of cattle was passing over it, the bridge collapsed.

The hopes of many investors were shattered with it. The faith that had been placed in the strength and security of a suspension bridge was destroyed in a few terrible minutes. Only the hardiest adventurers had any heart left now to push the idea of a suspension bridge across the Ohio.

Yet the times were favorable. Credit, if not money, was readily available. Ever since 1849 the country had been growing more prosperous. The precious tide of gold from California was like new blood in the arteries of trade. By 1854 and 1855 there was a real boom on all sides. It was the first great railroad boom. Every investor in the country foresaw a fortune for himself in railroad stock. A mere bridge seemed to lack the appeal which made the railroads so attractive. Utterly beyond reason, money poured into the offices of the railroad companies; and, boom or no boom, the Bridge Company had a hard time in selling stock.

The Covington and Cincinnati Bridge Company had been formed, chartered by the States of Kentucky and Ohio. It had employed an engineer, John A. Roebling, to draw up a plan for the bridge. And there it had stopped. How the next ten years passed has been a story of constant discouragement. But early in 1856 the company turned another corner. On February 5 a new man was elected to the Board of Directors, Amos Shinkle. From that date on, a different fortune followed the bridge.

AMOS SHINKLE

AMOS SHINKLE, the stranger in the Board of Directors of the Bridge Company, was no stranger either to Cincinnati or Covington. He had lived in Covington for ten years, and businessmen on both sides of the river were his friends.

White Oak Creek runs into the Ohio River just above Higginsport, in Brown County, Ohio. On a farm in its narrow, winding valley, Amos Shinkle was born, August 11, 1818. He was the son of Peter Shinkle, a local lumber merchant. When he was sixteen, Amos set up in the business for himself. It was not a great success. Next he opened a store in Higginsport, the flourishing little landing on the Ohio. His luck this time was no better than before.

At the age of eighteen, with seventy-five cents in his pocket, Amos Shinkle left home and came to Cincinnati. There he found work as a cook on a flatboat. The boat took him to New Orleans. Then he had to find his way back to Cincinnati.

Shinkle made the long trip down the river again and again, down the Ohio, down the Mississippi to the great seaport of the South. The boatmen with whom he traveled used to start at

Marietta with a load of salt from the Great Salt Bend of the Ohio. Along the way, they traded salt to farmers for cattle, and traded the cattle at Cincinnati for picks and shovels, nails and axes. All down the river they traded goods, until they finally came to New Orleans.

There they sold their cargo for cash, and frequently sold the boat, too, for what the timber in it would bring. Five or six trips a year, at most, could be made down the river.

Shinkle came back sometimes by sea, shipping from New Orleans to Baltimore, and then crossing the mountains by way of the Chesapeake and Ohio Canal, or the old Cumberland Road. Sometimes he made the trip back by land. In that case, he rode with a party, for there were long stretches of wilderness in Louisiana, Mississippi, and Tennessee still infested with thieves and Indians.

On these long trading voyages cash was not abundant. Most of the business was done by barter. But from each trip Shinkle managed to save a little. Finally he bought a flatboat of his own. He loaded lumber in eastern Kentucky and took it down to New Orleans. There it was bought to build ships or houses. Once more Shinkle tried his luck with a store, this time a grocery. But good fortune again refused to follow him.

Sometime between 1838 and 1844, Shinkle received from Governor Wilson Shannon a commission as first lieutenant of artillery in the Eighth Division of Ohio Militia. In the Mexican War

AMOS SHINKLE
President, 1866-1892

he offered his services and his company. But the war was so brief hostilities had ended before he was mustered in.

Shinkle's luck with boats was quite a different matter. As a merchant or army man, he never seemed to get very far. With boats, he had steady success. He joined with his brother now, and the two young men ran a steamer, the *Governor Breathitt,* from Cincinnati up the river to Ripley, Ohio. As the business improved, he married and settled down in Higginsport. There his only son Bradford was born in 1845. The Shinkle brothers stayed in this business until 1846.

Amos Shinkle had his eye on something new. He saw that steamboat traffic was the road to success in the Ohio Valley. Boats needed coal. Cincinnati was the logical place for boats to refuel, for it was the most important shipping center in a thousand miles of riverways. But the Cincinnati wharves were too valuable in shipping merchandise to be used for loading fuel. Across the river lay Covington. It was a new city, and it was growing rapidly. In 1840 there were barely two thousand people in Covington; by 1845 there were more than twice as many. In August, 1846, Shinkle moved to Covington, and there he set up as a coal dealer. In the fifteen years before the Civil War, from 1846 to 1861, Shinkle made a fortune in supplying coal to steamboats. By 1861 he had three boats of his own.

Through his business, Shinkle readily came to see the paramount importance of commerce and transportation. He was interested financially in the building of turnpikes: he had had many experiences on the long trip down to New Orleans, with river pirates, and on the long ride back, with thieves and Indians. He knew, too, the importance of bringing interior rural districts into closer touch with river ports, to stimulate commerce. The efforts to build a bridge to Cincinnati must have touched his imagination. Finally, in February, 1856, he bought his stock in the bridge company, and was elected a director.

A NEW SPIRIT

FROM the day Shinkle was elected to the board, February 5, 1856, a new spirit entered into the company. A committee was appointed immediately to prepare by-laws for the company. In the record-breaking time of two days the committee was ready to report. On February 7, seventeen by-laws were brought in and adopted.

At the same meeting, the board adopted three resolutions. Two of them were to have immediate effect of the greatest consequences:

"Resolved, That a committee of two directors be appointed whose duty it shall be to visit the Legislatures of Ohio and Kentucky, to solicit any alterations in the charter that may be thought desirable by this board, and that such committee may have the privilege of procuring such aid and assistance as may be requisite in securing such amendments"; and,

"Resolved, That the committees appointed to wait on the Legislature of Ohio be instructed to ask the reduction of the span of the bridge to not less than one thousand feet, and also that the capital stock may be increased to $700,000—and further to ask the Legislature of Kentucky to grant an increase of the capital stock to $700,000."

The new committees set to work at once. Within three weeks, on February 25, 1856, the Kentucky Legislature passed an amendment to the charter authorizing the increase of capital stock to $700,000. The city of Covington was permitted to subscribe $100,000 of this amount, to be paid for by the issue of municipal bonds. As the original Kentucky charter had made no restrictions on the length of the bridge, there was no need for further change.

Meanwhile, on March 29, the Ohio Legislature passed an amendment of the same sort. It permitted the capital stock to be increased to $700,000, and authorized the reduction of the bridge span below the former fourteen-hundred foot length, but not to be less than one thousand feet. At the same time, however, the Ohio Legislature required that the bridge be raised still higher, to not less than one hundred and twenty-two feet above the surface of the river at low water mark.

No time was lost in going after new capital. At the meeting on February 7, two days after Shinkle's election, the board decided to re-open the books of the company for stock subscription. The same day, the board resolved to appoint a committee to solicit stock subscriptions, with power to employ persons to assist them in the work.

For the remainder of the month the old board did almost nothing; but on March 3, 1856, a completely new Board of Directors was elected. Only

Amos Shinkle, the most recent addition to the old group, was carried over. Richard H. Ranson, connected with the Kentucky Central Railroad, became the new president; Amos Shinkle, Henry Bruce, and John W. Finnell represented Covington. Miles Greenwood and Thomas Phillips, both iron manufacturers, and Joseph C. Butler, a wholesale grocer and commission merchant, represented the Ohio side on the board.

A few days later, on March 15, Greenwood and Shinkle were appointed to find the number of foot passengers, wagons, drays, carriages, buggies, cattle, and hogs that crossed the river on the Covington and Cincinnati ferry boats at Walnut Street. They were to station men at some convenient point for one week, to take the count. A week later, their report was in.

On April 5, another committee was appointed to wait upon Captain Ayers of the Newport Ferry, to get a statement from him of the amount of crossing and the receipts for a six-months' period.

At the same time, President Ranson wrote to John Roebling, inviting him to come to Cincinnati, with expenses paid by the company. Roebling arrived in Cincinnati on April 16, after an absence of almost ten years. He met with a committee from the board, and presented a communication in relation to the "Practicability and probable cost of a Suspension Bridge across the Ohio River." The report was in turn presented by the committee to the board.

Next, President Ranson prepared "an appeal

to the people for material aid for the bridge." On the instruction of the board, he combined with it a statement of his own and the communication which had just been received from Roebling, as well as the Report of the Committee on the Crossings at the Ferry. One thousand copies were printed by Munger and Croninger, and distributed in Cincinnati and Covington.

On the first day of July, the president was instructed by the board to try to get railroads in Cincinnati to subscribe to stock. At the same time he wrote to Roebling, stating "that this board had sufficient stock subscribed to justify them in making a contract with an engineer and that said board would be glad to have a further conference with him." The newspapers carried an account of the good news on the same day, and everyone looked forward to the early commencement of the work.

So bright were the prospects that the board decided to look into the matter of getting stone for the towers. Their first move was to investigate the possibilities of using the stone in the locks and dams on the Licking River.

Roebling offered his proposition two weeks later for engineering the construction of the Covington and Cincinnati Bridge. It was received by the board on July 14.

While negotiations on this contract were under way, the company decided to receive bids from stone and timber men for furnishing materials for the foundations of the towers. At the same time, a committee was appointed to draw up a proposition for one Mr. Wiggins and others, to buy the right-of-way for the Covington and Cincinnati Bridge on the Ohio side.

A temporary deadlock with Mr. Wiggins was reached in a very short time. President Ranson returned to the board, and reported under the circumstances "that he deemed it inexpedient to make the offer, from intimations he had received that satisfied him Mr. Wiggins would not accept of it, when the president and the committee appointed on the 23d inst. were discharged from having anything to do in the premises."

Then the company began to call on the stock subscribers. On July 30, the first call of 10% ($10) on each share was made, payable on or before September 5. The money began at last to come in. During August further arrangements were made for securing stone, timber, sand, and cement for construction work.

Negotiations with Roebling were going along smoothly but a bit slowly. On August 4, Roebling, who was now working on a bridge at Waterloo, Black Hawk County, Iowa, offered another set of terms. They were received by the board a little over a week later. As Roebling had other work to do at Chicago and Niagara Falls, he suggested coming to Cincinnati about the first of September. The Bridge Company were by this time too enthusiastic to take a chance of any further delay. President Ranson went in person to Iowa to see Roebling and complete the arrangements. On August 18, 1856, the contract was entered into between Roebling and the Bridge Company. After more than ten years, the Bridge Company had at last secured an engineer who could build the bridge they wanted. Roebling had secured an opportunity to build the greatest bridge in his career.

Under the terms of the contract, both Roebling and the company expected that the bridge would be completed in three years, or four at most. The contract was to continue in force four years from September 1, 1856, provided the bridge should not be finished sooner.

At the end of August, 1856, everything was ready to begin work on the great structure.

BUILDING THE TOWERS

ALMOST ten years to the day after Roebling submitted his first *Report and Plan,* work was begun on the bridge. "By a wise resolution of the Board of Managers," Roebling wrote, "the work was not to be commenced before a bona fide cash subscription of $300,000 had been secured. Contrary to my expectations, this subscription was rapidly obtained; and in view of the promising state of the river, it was concluded to forthwith commence the foundation work."

A more suitable moment could scarcely have been found. By September 1, $314,000 had been subscribed in stock. A long, dry summer had left the river lower than it had been for seventeen years, since the great drought of 1839. But so swiftly had success come upon the reorganized Bridge Company that few of the necessary preparations were complete. There were no materials on hand, though bids had been received and accepted; and much to Roebling's disgust there was no machinery and no effective pumps.

At the meeting of the board on September 2, there was more business to be attended to than ever before. President Ranson and Mr. Roebling were requested to visit Dayton, Ohio, and other places to examine stone for the company. Greenwood and Roebling were authorized to buy engines, pumps, and hoisting apparatus. The president, Shinkle, and Roebling, were appointed to take the necessary steps to buy the stone at Six Mile Lock, on the Licking River. A committee was appointed to obtain suitable barrels for cement. And, finally, the president was authorized to draw on the treasurer for the first expenditures, $2,500, to pay off the hands engaged at that time in excavating at the river.

After examining the Covington shore, the engineer, Mr. Gower, reported that there was but little difficulty in finding a good foundation there. A heavy bed of coarse sand, mixed with gravel, was found above the blue limestone rock bottom. Above the sand the surface layer was composed of the original clay bottom of the river. This clay also formed the visible river bank.

Work was commenced by the contracting firm of Dawson, Mattoon, and Messer. Originally stone masons from Springfield, Massachusetts, they were now one of the leading construction firms in Cincinnati. The Bridge Company had arranged to have them furnish the stone, cut, and lay it for the erection of the two towers.

On the Covington side of the river, the excavation for the foundations proceeded easily and quickly. It was finished within less than three weeks. On Monday, September 22, the first timbers for the superstructure were laid down there. Heavy oak logs were hewed square and laid so as to form a solid platform. A second layer was then laid crosswise over the first, and the two were fastened together with iron bolts. Two layers of these oak timbers had already been laid down for the foundations on the Covington side by October 11, and preparations were being made for the third layer.

On the Cincinnati side there was a different situation. The original clay bottom of the river had to some extent been washed away. More recently it had been filled up again by the dirt obtained from cellar excavations in the city. In this artificial bank the excavation for the Cincinnati tower was commenced about the first of September.

When the Cincinnati excavation was begun, a strong oak sheet piling was driven into the mud along the river front to guard against the pressure of water. This, together with the solid embankment, proved an efficient coffer dam on the river side. In a few days workmen had dug down to the level of the river. Owing to the low stage and slight volume of water, it gave them no trouble at all.

But by the great depth and extent of the foundation, most of the wells along the rising ground back of Cincinnati, were laid dry. "We drained their supplies," Roebling explained, "and had to pump them out; and this copious influx came from a quarter totally unexpected."

During September the river fortunately continued to fall still lower. The autumn rains fell off. The Newport ferry boat had great difficulty in crossing, and finally had to stop. On the 18th, the *Belle* went aground, and passengers had to cross the river in light skiffs. By the end of the month, bars and ridges were plainly visible in the channel itself, opposite Main Street. Mail boats were still able to make regular trips up and down the river; but the water continued to fall during the whole month.

By mid-September the workmen had dug as deep as low water mark on the Cincinnati side. Water from the river began to flow into the excavation, seriously interfering with the work. On the 15th, Engineer Gower placed an engine in position to operate a steam pump, which he expected would remedy the problem. Contracts were meanwhile made for limestone, oak and pine timber, and another pump.

At the end of September the chief difficulty was still the flow of water into the excavation on the Cincinnati side. Pumps worked by steam engines were kept in constant motion. They threw out tremendous quantities of water. But they were inadequate. Roebling saw that the want of powerful pumps was a serious drawback. It threatened to defeat the enterprise at the very outset. The city was full of steamboat pumps, it was true. But they were of such small dimensions, and of such a type of construction that they were of no account in these operations.

"Raising clean water is an easy process," Roebling said, "but to raise large masses of soft mud and sand is not so easy. After experimenting and losing a few precious weeks in an endeavor to work some patent rotary pumps, which utterly failed, we came very near to a complete halt. There was no time to get proper steam pumps of large dimensions constructed at any of the shops in Cincinnati, nor could we expect them in time from the East; every day's loss was irreparable—and so we were thrown back upon our own resources."

Instead of continuing the excavation, the contractors were now thinking of driving spikes in order to secure a good foundation. This might delay the work, but if only the river would continue as low as it was then, both piers might yet be built above high water mark before winter. Optimistic reports were given to the newspapers, for the public was curious about the progress. But it was hard to hide the fact that work was almost at a standstill.

During October public interest was taken up with the excitement of a presidential election campaign. The new Republican Party was running its first national candidate, John Fremont. At the election early in November, the Democratic candidate, Buchanan, proved an easy victor, and the country settled back to its normal routine.

In Cincinnati and Covington interest swung back almost immediately to the bridge. The *Enquirer* reported on November 7 that seven or eight layers of heavy timber had been laid down on the Covington side, and stone masons were already at work there preparing the stone. By the middle of the month enough additional timbers had been laid to make thirteen courses altogether. The whole mass was then made solid by a plentiful use of concrete. Above this, two courses of heavy masonry were already set in place. Then the contractors looked forward to the possibility of a rise in the river before the beginning of December. They built a coffer dam around the work, making it completely water tight. Thus, even if a rise in the river should occur, work might proceed without interruption. A large number of stone cutters were busy on the spot, shaping huge masses of rock to suit the needs of the masons. On all sides, hope was fervent that rain would hold off.

On the Cincinnati side, however, there were still great difficulties in the way of securing a proper foundation. The constant flow of water into the excavation retarded the progress of operations.

The fall rains were at last beginning in November, and the river was gradually creeping back up the shores. Every day, every hour indeed counted now, as Roebling cast about for some way to meet the situation. At last he determined to build the necessary pumps himself. He made four large square box pumps of three-inch pine plank. These he set up vertically in pairs, with one pair working at a time.

The pumps were propelled by chains connected with one of the engines of the *Champion No. 1*. This was a powerful tugboat, owned by Amos Shinkle, which was lying close to the landing. The pumps worked effectively, and never once failed. They threw mud and sand as effectively as pure water, and discharged forty gallons at each lift. No difficulty was now experienced by the workmen from the flow of water, and excavation proceeded rapidly, day and night, until all the clay and sand was removed.

Then, much to the relief of everyone, the rains stopped. The river had risen four feet since the beginning of November; now it fell back once more.

With the surface layer of clay and sand removed, a deep layer of coarse sand and gravel was now exposed on the Cincinnati side. Soundings were next made by driving long iron bars down to the limestone shale beneath, which proved to be about twelve feet lower. A depth of over twelve feet below extreme low water was reached, and the question arose, whether to go to the rock, to drive piling, or to lay down a solid timber platform.

"A compact bed of gravel," Roebling explained, "if left undisturbed, and protected against undermining and washing, stands next to a solid rock foundation, provided that unequal settling is guarded against. Had this tower been located inside of low water mark, I should have decided upon going down to the rock, although one season's loss would have been the consequence. Piling I considered inferior to the plan adopted, say nothing of the loss of time. It was therefore decided to stop at the gravel, and build a solid timber foundation up to low water mark, thence to commence the masonry. If the timber could be obtained in time in sufficient quantity, the success of this kind of foundation was much more certain to be achieved, and with less risk and cost, than any other plan."

There the enormous hole gaped, eighty-two feet along the length of the river, and fifty-two feet wide, waiting for the foundations to be built. It was not empty for long. Within a few days the sand and gravel bottom was hidden by a flooring of oak timbers, just as on the Covington side. By the middle of November the crowd of spectators which constantly surrounded the foundations had watched five more tiers of heavy timbers laid in place. Eighty hands were now constantly at work, trying to bring the Cincinnati construction up to schedule. The immense pumps connected with the engines of Shinkle's *Champion No. 1* kept the excavation clear of water, and work progressed rapidly.

The last of the ten courses of timber was secured on the Cincinnati side two days before the end of November; and the foundation was leveled off to receive the first course of masonry.

Up to this time, the contractors, Dawson, Mattoon, and Messer, had been favored to an unprecedented extent by the low state of the river. It would have been hazardous to expect the low water to continue. The river was "still going down, down, down," as the newspapers reported it; and deckhands, cooks, and chambermaids who worked on the boats were in distress for want of work. But the season had now arrived when a sudden rise of ten to twenty feet would be the result of one week's steady rain.

Materials were therefore prepared for strong timber caissons. These were built, twenty feet high, around the top course of the foundation, well braced, and embanked all around. The planks were all jointed and caulked, and so was the floor of the foundation.

Thus prepared, a rise of twenty feet in the river could not interfere with the work. Sure enough, on the day after Thanksgiving the late fall rains began. In a few hours the river was beginning to rise, ever so slightly. The rains continued, the water rose, and in a few more days river traffic began to pick up. Early in December the rise in the river began to retard the work somewhat; but the contractors were in excellent spirits. They were confident of their ability to put the work out of all danger from this source within the next few weeks.

Much to the pleasant surprise of everyone, the early and midpart of December proved to be mild and fair. Hundreds of citizens gathered daily to watch the work on the towers.

On the Covington side, enough masonry had been laid above the timbers to take the pier well out of the reach of danger. In Cincinnati, several layers of stone had been laid down by the middle of the month.

The achievements of the first fall's work were well secured by the time the season came to a close. Altogether, some thirty-two thousand cubic feet of masonry had been put in place.

"Since the time when the first symptoms of an earnest intention to erect a bridge over the Ohio between Cincinnati and Covington manifested themselves," a newspaper now observed, "there has been a steady and healthful increase in the value of real estate in Covington. It is beyond a doubt that the great value of landed property in Cincinnati renders it ineligible for manufactures. This is caused by the necessity, which is every day becoming more apparent, of room for business houses. Commerce is slowly, but surely, grasping every available spot within our city and turning it to account to swell the number of her marts. Stores and warehouses rent at enormous sums, and manufacturers, if an eligible location could be found, would readily yield up the places now occupied by these factories to the merchant and his wares, and conduct their own operations on less costly ground. Covington offers such places in abundance, but the great difficulty so far has been the inconvenience experienced in crossing the river. The new bridge, when completed, will obviate this difficulty by affording means of speedy transit from one side to the other. . . . It is also thought . . . that many of our wealthy citizens will select Covington as a place of residence when the bridge is finished. . . ."

Throughout the entire fall the Board of Directors held meetings twice a month instead of once, so great was the amount of business to be looked after. Receiving and spending money was a completely new item on their agenda, and during these months it was set out in great detail in their minutes. Up to December 1, 1856, total disbursements amounted to just over $17,000.

The receipts of the company were timed to meet current needs. After the first call on the stock subscription in July, four more calls of ten per cent each per share were made: on September 17, November 18, December 21, and January 30. A steady supply of cash was thus available to pay for materials and labor employed.

There was, of course, the usual quota of trouble as well. A contract had been made for the right of way with the irascible Samuel Wiggins. This was concluded on July 30, 1856. But there was now the problem of getting Mr. Wiggins to have his tenants move from the property which the Bridge Company required. In November it turned out that there was, indeed, some question as to whether the ground involved had actually been in Wiggins' power to sell. There seems to have been an incumbrance on the property dating from almost twenty-five years before. A dispute arose between Wiggins and the Bridge Company over their respective rights to the property which required much time and attention.

BUILDING TOWERS: THE SECOND SEASON

AFTER the close of the first building season, the Bridge Company revised its plans for the coming year. On Christmas Day, 1856, they concluded new arrangements with Dawson, Mattoon, and Messer. The contractors agreed to furnish the stone, cut, and lay it, for the erection of the two towers. The Bridge Company was to supply all the cement and sand needed for the mason work, as well as all the steam power and machinery necessary for hoisting and laying the stone. This machinery consisted of one steam engine for each tower, and derricks and hoisting apparatus for each engine.

Work under this contract was to begin the following spring, as soon as the weather and the state of the river would permit. It was to continue so that 15,000 to 20,000 perches (375,-000 to 500,000 cubic feet) of stone would be laid during the 1857 season. The rest of the work was to be completed by December 1, 1858. No stones were to be laid, however, in weather which the engineers should decide to be unsuitable.

This contract was to be subject to be varied by "unavoidable calamities, such as epidemics, and uncontrollable contingencies, such as the state of the weather or of the river." If either the company or the contractors ever suspected the calamity which would come eight months later, it was never hinted in this contract.

The winter of 1856-57 was a terrible one, and long remembered in Cincinnati. The Ohio River froze over a week after New Years', on January 8. Long, instense cold remained without breaking, week after week. Boats of any sort found it impossible to reach the city. Almost all commerce was ended, except the bit carried on by the new railroad lines. Coal was next to impossible to buy, and the price kept climbing higher. The poor were in great distress, with no fuel for their stoves. In time, coal could not be had at any price; and there was a threatened shortage of food. Even those with money to buy felt the effects of the bitter weather.

Early in February, rains commenced in central Ohio. In a few days the Little Miami, which enters the Ohio just above Cincinnati, was in flood. Within twenty-four hours the cold began to yield. The mercury rose from zero to the thawing point, and climbed still further.

The river ice began to grind and shift, rocking uneasily. It began to move. On Thursday morning, February 5, the ice broke. The terrible scenes which followed brought tragic losses to the citizens. Boats which had been locked fast in the ice were splintered or torn apart. Some were forced down beneath the floes, others raised high over the jammed ice, only to plunge, crashing into the jagged mass. During this whole pleasant day of warm, gentle winds and spring-like freshness, the people of the river cities stood by helplessly watching the awful spectacle. Floods which followed only prolonged the disaster.

As winter passed into spring, high water continued with almost no interruption, from March to April, from April to May, and from May to June. Not until July did the stage fall low enough to permit recommencement of work on the towers. This year the work was concerned almost entirely with building up the great cable piers.

The stone used at the core of the massive piers came from far up the Ohio River. Two hundred miles above Cincinnati, between the Muskingum and the Scioto, great sandstone bluffs overlooked the river on either side. Thomas Ewing, one of Ohio's senators and one time Secretary of the Treasury, had often looked at the cliffs; and he it was who had told Roebling about the stone in the early days, when the first bridge plans were drawn up.

When Roebling finally came to Cincinnati to direct the construction of the bridge, he had already decided to use this Buena Vista sandstone, or freestone. "I preferred for the lower portions of the masonry," he said, "the petroleum variety of the Buena Vista quarries, because of their greater strength and impregnation with petroleum, which latter condition promised a greater resistance to the action of the water."

The first twenty-five feet of the towers above the foundation, however, required special treatment. This part, up to the top of the first offset, would be constantly exposed to the action of the current. Roebling decided, therefore, to have it faced with a good quality of limestone.

Various stones were tried. A few boatloads of shell marble from the quarries below Madison, Indiana, were secured as samples; but it was impossible to use this because it could not be obtained in an adequate supply. Other limestone from Ohio and Indiana quarries was examined. Finally the principal supply was taken from Dayton, Ohio. This Dayton limestone had first been introduced for building purposes in Cincinnati around 1842. Old St. Peter's Cathedral on Plum Street was the first important building in which it was used.

Above the first offsets, the towers were of sandstone. The faces of the blocks were left rough, as they came out of the quarry near Portsmouth, Ohio. A heavy draft was run around the margin of each stone before it was moved into position. Thus the surfaces of the towers had, as Roebling observed, "a massive look quite suitable to their function."

From July to November almost the whole efforts of the company were directed toward this work. Never before in this part of the country had such enormous masses of stone been raised and set at such great heights. It was a new problem, and one that exercised the skill of the engineers.

Animal power would not have been enough to meet the tasks of the second season, so two steam engines had been set up, one on each side of the river, to supply power. Four hoisting barrels, worked by friction clutches, were then connected with each steam engine. The raising and setting of the stones was done by masted derricks, secured in their positions by wire rope guys.

Work proceeded in this manner through the summer and fall of 1857 with little interruption. Early in November high water began to interfere with the work; and when the river showed no signs of falling, work was finally brought to a close for the season shortly after the middle of the month. During this second season of construction, about 166,000 cubic feet of stone had been laid, bringing the total to almost 200,000 cubic feet.

But in the meantime, the Bridge Company ran into more serious difficulties than high water or cold weather. The $314,000 of stock originally subscribed by September, 1856, had been increased during the rest of that year and 1857 to a total of $413,300, still far short of the $700,000 authorized.

The first call on this subscription was made in July, 1856. Later calls through March, 1857, were expected to bring in about sixty per cent of the whole subscription. But almost from the outset there was difficulty in collecting the payments. In October the names of delinquent stockholders were presented at a meeting of the board. Steps were taken after the November meeting to make collections from these subscribers. Finally in January, 1857, the president was directed to institute suits against delinquents.

It was apparent, too, with half the capital already called in by the end of February, 1857, that additional stock sales would be necessary. President Ranson packed his suitcases in March and set off for New York to do what he could. He returned from the east in April—empty-handed.

Spring was already here. The river might at any time fall to a low stage. The company should be ready to begin work again at a moment's notice. In payment of installments due on stock subscription, the board agreed to take notes and bills of exchange at short date.

The Bridge Company was by no means the only business faced with this trouble. Demand for capital to invest far exceeded the supply immediately available. California miners were literally pouring tons of gold into the pockets of the nation. They had been doing it ever since 1849. But the enthusiasm of promoters grew at an even faster rate. Especially in this new, raw West, where no one had yet had time to accumulate any capital reserves, this shortage was acute. The eight-year upswing to prosperity was approaching a climax; by 1856 and 1857 the shortage of actual cash was pressing hard on the heels of investors. The Bridge Company and scores of other concerns were all in difficulty trying to make collections.

Money had to be found somewhere to pay contractors and laborers for material and work. When Ranson came back from New York, reporting complete lack of success, he proposed to the board that they take over the City of Covington Bridge Bonds. These were the bonds issued by Covington to raise money to pay for her $100,000 subscription to capital stock. They had never been sold; hence, there was no money in the Covington treasury to pay for the stock. Now the Bridge Company was willing to take the bonds instead of money, and try to sell them.

A special meeting was held four days later to handle the financial problem. A committee which had already been named brought in its report on the issuing of bonds. They recommended, first, that the president be authorized to issue $500,000 ten per cent fifteen-year bonds; second, that a mortgage should be issued with all stock, real estate, and materials as backing. The seventh call on the stock subscription was then made, to be paid by the middle of June; and some further steps were taken to secure the payments on the other six calls due from a number of delinquent subscribers.

During the early part of May, most of the attention of the board was taken up with the problem of the Covington Bridge bonds. Committees and subcommittees on both sides were active. Finally President Ranson met the Committee of Ways and Means of the Covington City Council and completed the transaction. He received from them ninety bonds of $1,000 each, in payment of the balance due on the city's subscription to stock. The bonds were then deposited in a Covington bank; and Ranson was given authority to sell, hypothecate, or pledge the bonds received.

Ranson went once more to New York to see what could be done with the Covington bonds. Only worse trouble than before waited for him. When he returned to Cincinnati to report to the board in mid-July, he had not been able to dispose of a single bond. Another call for payment on stock subscriptions was made; yet the same day the company accepted a mortgage on some Covington real estate in part payment of a previous call. At that meeting the secretary of the board resigned. Five weeks later, while construction was still going on, the treasurer resigned.

The storm had broken. On the afternoon of August 24, 1857, news came by telegraph from New York of a bank failure: the New York office of the Ohio Life Insurance and Trust Company had closed its doors. It was soon known that the main branch, in Cincinnati, would not open the next day. Only two days before the stock of the trust company had sold at ninety-eight. The failure was totally unexpected. But things had gone so far that nothing could now stop a general collapse.

THE OHIO BRIDGE

In a few brief weeks insurance companies and brokers, first in Cincinnati, then in New York and Philadelphia, and soon all over the world, were closing their doors. The panic of 1857, like the great panic just twenty years before, swept across the country with hurricane violence. Railroads went into bankruptcy east and west, north and south. Factories preparing for the normal fall upturn were swiftly shut down. Nothing but gloom could be found anywhere. Businessmen seemed to feel that the country was doomed to the despair of the "hungry forties," that long, dull depression after the panic of 1837, when no enterprise had flourished. The prosperity from 1850 to 1856 was just an illusion, it seemed; and now the illusion had vanished.

While prosperity might disappear overnight, the stone of the great bridge towers was lasting stuff. Those were towers which would stand, regardless of prosperity or panic, without respect for ice or flood.

WORK COMES TO A STOP

ONE misfortune after another dogged the steps of the bridge builders; but they were not men to give up without a fight. Banks might fail and railroads go into receivership; New York brokers might refuse to take bridge stock and city bonds; subscribers might fail by the carload to pay the calls on their stock subscriptions; but as long as there was a fighting chance, the Bridge Company intended to go on.

At the beginning of 1858, the whole amount of stock subscribed was a little over $400,000. The amount received on this account, including $90,000 in bonds, was about $275,000. With some other miscellaneous receipts, the company had taken in altogether about $290,000. It had spent some $193,000; and had on hand a balance of about half that much.

Money came in slowly, and sometimes not at all in the winter of 1857-1858. In the very teeth of the panic, the last two calls for payment on stock were made, on September 4 and October 7, 1857. Desperately, in October the Board of Directors resolved to issue single certificates of stock, when so required, or when they could be sold in that way. But it was not a good season for selling stock or raising money.

During that winter the president and Board of Directors tried threats, persuasion, and negotiation, all without success. In February, they finally secured an amendment from the Kentucky Legislature which permitted them to issue bonds and to sell additional stock. The Ohio Legislature passed a similar act in April. The plan was to issue $300,000 of preferred stock, which would be guaranteed the first six per cent of net income. It was the first time a preferred stock issue had been suggested; Roebling urged that the bridge would easily pay ten per cent. But no one offered to buy the stock.

In April, 1858, the company tried once more to raise money on the bonds which Covington had given in payment of her stock subscription. First they asked for an election in Covington on the question of levying a one-half per cent tax for three years. This, it was estimated, should raise the $90,000 which could be used to redeem the city bonds. The election was held, and the proposition was voted down.

Next, the board tried once again to sell the bonds. A meeting of stockholders was held, and the situation explained. The stockholders adopted a preamble and two resolutions expressing their policy:

"Believing the early completion of the bridge will open a cheap, convenient, and uninterrupted avenue on a great line of travel and be of immense advantage to the public, as well as pecuniary benefit to the stockholders; and having undiminished confidence in the integrity and discretion of the directors of the company, it is hereby declared to be the opinion of this meeting:

"1st, That the interest of all concerned requires the immediate and vigorous prosecution of work on the bridge;

"2d, That in order to effect this the directors are advised to avail themselves of all means in their power, within the limits of the charter; and as one step in this direction they offer for sale the bonds of the City of Covington issued to the company on such terms as they may think advisable, either to the stockholders or to any other person or persons in this or in any other market . . . ."

It was an announcement of desperation. The company had no choice, it seemed, but to dispose of the bonds for whatever they might yield. Very few could be sold for cash. A few were accepted by creditors who saw no other way of getting immediate payment. But more than half, fortunately, were disposed of to contractors in exchange for promises of materials or labor in the future, as might be required. By the middle of May this transaction was completed.

Because of high water, the workmen were unable to reach the base of the towers until early in the summer. About July first, however, the machinery was moved into place, and operations started.

At the time the Cincinnati tower was somewhat higher than the Covington tower. In order to keep expenditures within the limits of the company's ability to pay, the contractors agreed to confine work to one side of the river at a time.

During the season, which lasted until December, most of the work was done on the Kentucky side. Another hundred thousand cubic feet of stone were laid, bringing the total for the three seasons to about 312,000 cubic feet, or 12,000 perches. There were still 20,000 perches of masonry to be built. By the end of the season, the Cincinnati tower had reached a height of forty-seven feet; the Covington tower rose thirty feet higher.

Toward the end of November, the Bridge Company suffered a severe loss. The sudden death of President Richard Ranson deprived them of his experience, judgment, and inspiration. For almost three years President Ranson had guided the company through both success and adversity with a steady hand. His death was keenly felt by his associates. Miles Greenwood and Henry Bruce filled the remainder of his last term of office.

Early in 1859, the company tried once again to sell additional stock. At first the prospect was encouraging. But, abruptly, the Covington and Lexington Railroad was sold, a failure; and the City of Covington found its revenues so diminished that in September it defaulted on the interest payment on the bridge bonds. The prospect turned once more into utter hopelessness.

It was with a sad optimism that the directors,

early in 1860, drew up their Annual Report for 1859. In common with other stockholders, they wrote, they deeply regretted that a successful progress of work on the bridge could not be reported. Material and labor require money, and their efforts during the past season "to secure that essential," as they wrote, had met with poor success. The year 1859 had come and gone, and nothing had been done on the bridge.

After recounting the long tale of disappointments and failures of the preceding fourteen months, they recalled with a modest pride that the project for an Ohio bridge was basically sound, necessary, and wise:

"Notwithstanding the discredit to which the Covington and Cincinnati Bridge stock, in common with others, is now subject, we feel confident that its real merits will appear, and cause it to be sought for on account of its intrinsic value as a safe and profitable investment. A favorable move on the part of the City Council of Covington at this time would especially aid in bringing this stock into notice."

"The advantages of an unrestrained communication which a bridge will open between Covington and Cincinnati," they wrote, "are not of a questionable character—social and business intercourse will be promoted without detriment to either. The idea that the facility of a bridge communication will operate to the disadvantage of either Covington or Cincinnati is too preposterous to be entertained by a reflecting mind; as well might it be thought that improvement in the suburbs of a city would be injurious.

"Facilities of communications and business improvement necessarily benefit particular locations or individuals, but such benefit cannot be monopolized. The facility of a bridge communication must promote the interest of both cities. This reciprocal interest will insure permanence of profits to the bridge stock by inducing an intercourse between the two cities that will cause the bridge avenue to become a crowded thoroughfare. . . . Then the compactness, and small expense of its operation, the few agents required to manage the business, . . . make the investment equal to the most favorable real estate, both as to safety and income. Such stock cannot remain in the market without attracting the attention of persons seeking investment."

Such were the hopes the Bridge Company still held for the future. The obstacles were isolated and accidental. It was more than a year since the last stone had been laid in place on the towers and the machinery taken away; but the next spring, perhaps, would see another turn of events, and work might be started once more.

WAITING

AS THE year 1859 drew to a close, the directors of the Bridge Company took heart. It had not been such a bad year, they decided. No work had been done; no money had been found. But there was none of that spirit of panic which swept the country in 1857. Things had got no better; but they were no worse.

The company had spent all its money, or all but a small part. There stood the towers, giant unfinished monuments—worthless for the present, to be sure. But they would stand. Storm and flood, time and weather could scarcely touch them. As soon as times improved, work could be started just where it was left off.

"The most difficult portion of the bridge has been completed with much economy," the directors wrote in March, 1860. "The continued drought in the fall of 1856 was very favorable for excavating to a satisfactory depth for the foundation of the towers at comparatively small cost.

"Although the suspension of the work has not been of any disadvantage—the foundations and the masonry becoming more firmly settled, and set—the amount of capital laying idle, very naturally caused the stockholders to desire a recommencement of the work; which should be done at as early a day as practicable. But as a matter of prudence the work should not be resumed until an amount of fund were secured that will insure the completion of the structure, as the expense and waste in removing and replacing the machinery is too great to be often repeated. The mason work on the tower is now at a height that no ordinary rise in the river will cause the work to be suspended; so that when funds are obtained, the work on all portions of the structure should be urged forward to completion with all possible dispatch compatible with due regard to economy and thoroughness. To go on with the work in advance of the necessary means would endanger . . . all that has been so judiciously invested. By keeping within the means at command as has thus far been done, the company can wait a more favorable state of the stock market without serious injury."

The board completed its report, and recommended, for the present, a policy of waiting. A few days later, on March 5, 1860, the new Board of Directors was elected. John W. Finnell, of Covington, was elected as the first regular president after the death of Richard Ranson. More than half of the members, including three of the six directors, and the president of the board, were new.

The new board entered on the duties assigned them with no very flattering prospects for a speedy resumption of the work. The funds of the company were well-nigh exhausted. In consequence of the suspension of interest payments on the Covington bridge bonds, its credit was greatly impaired.

The board still hoped that the merit of the project would enable them to sell enough new stock to justify a resumption of the work. They believed that the real value of the improvement, if fairly presented to the public, would induce large subscriptions of stock. If this were not so, at least they hoped that those who had already subscribed and paid large sums in aid of the work, would come forward with additional subscriptions, rather than lose what they had already paid. Either result would justify them in beginning work again.

Toward the end of March, 1860, the board made an effort to bring the bridge closer to realization by cutting down on the anticipated cost. They decided to apply to the Ohio Legislature for an amendment to the charter which would allow them to lower the floor of the bridge from twelve to twenty feet. By making the bridge less costly to complete, it was hoped investors might be encouraged. A committee of three was appointed to carry out the resolution. But the project ended nowhere.

In all their expectations the directors were disappointed. They were wholly unable to interest capitalists either at home or abroad. The old stockholders failed to respond to the call upon them for new subscriptions sufficiently to enable the directors to go forward with the work.

The policy of the board was not to attempt to begin the work until enough stock was subscribed to insure the speedy completion of the structure, beyond any and all reasonable contingencies. They considered it idle and unjust to all parties interested to make any further expenditure, unless the amount at command were sufficiently large to complete the work.

A proposition was submitted to the people of Covington in May to authorize the construction of a street railway. It was to extend through certain streets of the city and across the bridge, connecting with a similar railway in Cincinnati. Street railways had just been invented, and the first ones in Cincinnati were built in 1859, when they immediately became extremely popular. The Bridge Company hoped by means of the proposed grant to secure a large subscription to the stock —such a subscription, indeed, as would secure the completion of the bridge. The citizens of Covington, however, thought otherwise; and the project was defeated by a heavy majority. The Board of Directors found themselves once more blocked in their efforts to raise new funds.

The spring passed into summer, and as July came on, the directors viewed the river front with discouragement. For three years it had been the scene of activity on the bridge. Now the bridge was so far forgotten that a Covington builder, Mr. Beatten, was preparing to put up a building in the midst of the proposed entrance to the bridge. Still with some hope, the directors sought court action, and prevented the obstacle.

Other efforts were made to interest capitalists and to sell stock, all unsuccessful. At last the old stock was offered at twenty-five per cent. There was no hope of attracting investors in this; it was a gesture of the hopelessness of ever securing anything of value from the investment.

As summer ripened into fall, the Bridge Company was caught in the grip of a national tragedy. No mere financial panic, no depression could have brought on the crisis which was now enfolding the company. The nation itself was in the throes of a crisis. It was being torn from top to bottom.

For almost half a century the two great sections, North and South, had been growing more self-conscious, and drifting farther apart. In a few brief weeks at the end of 1860 the last bond between them was suddenly broken, the bond of allegiance to one government and one flag. If Lincoln were elected, the Southern States promised, they would secede from the Union. In November, 1860, Lincoln was elected. Instantaneously a wild spirit of Southern patriotism swept across the land where cotton was king. The rest of the country looked on in bewildered amazement. With the future so mysterious, so unpredictable, there was not a chance in the world for any company to raise new funds.

Early in this crisis, the first week in December, the Board of Directors met to do what they could. Contractors were demanding to be paid. The accounts were long overdue; but there was no money in the safe. Nor was there any hope— not the slightest—that new funds would be forthcoming, or that the claims could be liquidated.

The only thing left was to issue bonds to their creditors. There was no other choice. An amendment passed in February, 1858, had given the company authority to issue bonds secured by a mortgage on the property rights, income, and franchise of the company; and the terms of contracts made since then included this provision. With heavy hearts, the board agreed to authorize the issue of bonds up to $400,000, for thirty years. Then they decided to call a meeting of the stockholders.

On December twentieth, five days before Christmas, the stockholders met to hear the news. President Finnell read a report on the state of affairs. He told them of the repeated efforts and failures of the company to raise money. The work was intrinsically as valuable as ever; but unless it could be completed, it was worthless. Finnell listed the assets and liabilities of the company. There was a large balance still due the company, he explained, but it would not be available unless work went on, for it was chiefly stock subscriptions payable in labor and materials.

"A very large proportion of the balance due on cash subscriptions is not collectible, and the present state of things in the financial world renders it even less valuable than we were led to believe it a few months since." That was his simple way of describing the utter chaos which prevailed in the national investment market.

Then Finnell discussed the bond situation. No bonds had as yet been issued, and the board hoped that the necessity for issuing them could be avoided. But the contractors were "importuning, nay demanding, the bonds in conformity to the contracts, and in the absence of any reasonable hope," he did not see "with what show of justice" they could be put off any longer.

The objection to issuing bonds was no mere prejudice. There was an immediate danger to the success of the whole undertaking. If a mortgage should be made and the bonds issued to the contractors, Finnell explained, there was no way to pay the accruing interest to Mr. Wiggins, or even to meet the coupons on the bonds as they matured. A failure to pay the coupons promptly would probably lead to a suit, foreclosure, and the sale of property and franchise.

There seemed to be no escape. Between the immediate claims of the contractors, which could not be met except by bonds, and the postponed but ultimate threat of foreclosure, the directors were unable to choose. In this difficulty they set the facts before the stockholders for their suggestions and action. That the stockholders might be perfectly free in their action, the Board of Directors tendered their resignations.

There was no surprise in the situation for the stockholders. They must have known for some time of the mounting difficulties. Yet they were as helpless to deal with the catastrophe as the directors.

For the moment they accepted and endorsed the report which President Finnell had just finished reading. They declined, however, to accept the resignation of the officers. They approved the management of affairs, and begged the directors to fill out their regular terms. They appointed a committee of five stockholders, outside of the board, to consider the report and "devise some plan to extricate the company from present embarrassment." After this, they adjourned to celebrate the holidays as best they might, resolving to meet one week later.

The stockholders met again two days after Christmas. Their committee had now worked out a plan for a new stock issue. It was in principle similar to the plan proposed by Roebling early in 1858. This time, however, the plan suggested the issuing of preferred stock at the full fifteen per cent dividend, instead of the six per cent which Roebling had advocated.

The need was desperate; for as the committee reported: "They find that the available assets of the corporation are not sufficient to pay the liabilities now due, and maturing within the next four or six months. They believe that unless some plan can be devised to raise funds a sale of the franchise and property of the company must take place within the period named."

The committee were by no means sure, they

announced, "that in the present disturbed condition of the financial world new subscriptions can be had, but they are encouraged to hope, if there shall be a restoration of quiet and confidence at an early day, that the scheme now presented may be successfully carried out . . ."

In the meantime, too, prices in general had moved upward from the levels of 1858. It was now apparent that the bridge could not be completed at a total cost of under $1,000,000. The amount of new stock to be issued was therefore suggested as $400,000. After some discussion, this sum was changed by amendment to $500,000.

The remedy proposed was a drastic one; but no other plan offered even came near to protecting the property and rights of the company. This one at least had the merit of looking forward to "a restoration of quiet and confidence." It was a choice between getting the work completed, even though on difficult terms, and losing all that had been invested.

In this final test, the stockholders met the challenge. The bridge had to be saved, that it might some day be finished. The preferred stock issue was approved, and the secretary was directed to procure the signatures of the present owners of stock, since their written consent was necessary to make such a new contract legal. As soon as four-fifths of the new stock should be subscribed, the directors were to recommence the work. Pending the outcome of this move, the stockholders now adjourned. They would wait to see what happened.

Meanwhile the directors proceeded with the necessary steps to carry this program into effect. A bill was drafted and submitted to the Kentucky Legislature, increasing the capital stock to $1,000,000. Half of this amount might be preferred stock. Subscription to the new stock was first to be opened to holders of the original stock. If they did not take it all up, it was to be opened to the public. The amendment was passed early in February, 1861. Two days later the board met, to make application to the Ohio Legislature for the same measure. The Ohio Legislature passed the act early in April.

During the winter of 1861 the question of bonds to pay the contractors was still in the air. In February and March the mortgage was drawn and executed, and bonds were issued. Only enough were issued, however, to meet the demands due under existing contracts. Special arrangements were later made to take care of the small payments due Mr. Wiggins.

At a meeting in April 10, 1861, a number of economy moves were made. The treasurer was thenceforth to receive no compensation, since his duties were "nominal." The secretary was to receive but $100 per year after May first. The offices of the company were to be given up after that same date; and the records were to be moved "to a place of safety."

Finally the stockholders met on April twenty-fifth to vote on the new amendments to the charter. In the election, all of the 1,932 shares represented voted in favor of accepting the amendments now passed by the two State Legislatures, and issuing the preferred stock. The measure was thus carried. During the remainder of the year, the company seemed powerless to take any further action. Till the last week of the year, the Board of Directors made not a move.

During this whole two years, the Bridge Company was waiting—not for a depression to be shaken off, not for the attractions of their project to interest investors; they were waiting to learn whether America was to be one nation or two; whether, when the bridge was built, there would be a South below the Ohio river to bind with its Northern neighbors.

Many years of bitter fighting, the more tragic because brothers took arms against each other, followed these months of suspense. It was long before quiet and confidence were restored to the nation—longer than the bridge had to wait. In the midst of war, the bridge was to be born again.

WAR

THE weeks of terrible suspense lengthened into months, the old year passed into the new, and winter into spring. The two great sections of the nation, already divided, stood in tense expectancy. Allegiance to a common flag was gone. Rivers flowing from north to south could not hold them together; railroads between the sections were wanting. The mighty bridge piers stood facing each other from opposite shores of the Ohio, ready to bind North and South, yet not connected by a single strand.

It was a warm spring evening just before the middle of April. The hedges were clothed in fresh green, though the locust trees were still black and naked. Singing along the telegraph wires came the fateful news. Southern troops had shelled a fort of the Federal Government. Three days later, President Lincoln called for seventy-five thousand volunteers, to serve three months in suppressing the rebellion.

Along the Ohio, fear and anxiety were twins. Kentucky was a Southern State; she lay below the Mason-Dixon Line; her farmers grew a Southern crop, tobacco, with slave labor. Would she join the Confederacy? Perhaps. Yet her ties with

Ohio and the North were strong. Perhaps they would prove too strong to be broken, after all. It was a critical hour.

The Confederacy had been completed by January, 1861. No more States seemed likely to secede. Months passed, and no move was made on either side. But when Lincoln called for troops, a new wave of Southern patriotism passed over Dixie. Virginia, North Carolina, and Tennessee withdrew from the Union. Kentucky was the child of old Virginia. Where would she go? Whichever side intervened with force would drive her into the opposing camp. It was for Kentucky to decide.

Thursday afternoon, April 18, 1861, less than a week after the firing on Fort Sumter, the citizens of Covington, Cincinnati, and Newport met in Covington to form a home guard for local protection. Committees were created; on the Covington committee were M. M. Benton, John W. Finnell, J. Banning, J. W. Baker, and Amos Shinkle, all connected with the Bridge Company. In the Cincinnati group were at least three more bridge men: Miles Greenwood, J. C. Butler, and Thomas Sherlock.

By the early part of May, the shotgun company thus formed in Covington adopted the title of Kenton Home Guards; and in a few days it had elected officers: four corporals, four sergeants, three lieutenants, and a captain, Amos Shinkle.

On July fourth, Captain Shinkle and his men

had a chance to demonstrate their loyalty. There was a great parade that day, and along the route, at the corner of Eleventh and Washington Streets, Shinkle's company passed the residence of Rev. Mr. Nicholson, who had lately arrived from Tennessee. In an upper window of Nicholson's house flew a Confederate flag. It was a deliberate provocation; and when the Home Guards reached the armory, they discussed what should be done about it. It came to a vote; and the men determined unanimously that the flag should be removed. A committee was sent back to Nicholson's to ask for the flag, and after a brief interview they obtained it.

Public excitement ran high over the incident for several days, and at last Shinkle himself was called on to make a statement. In words which left no doubt of his stand, he declared, "The day ... is fast approaching when every citizen of this commonwealth will necessarily be compelled to take his stand on one side or the other—either for the Constitution or no Constitution, Government or no Government, liberty or tyranny, and the sooner, in my humble judgment, this takes place the better."

The day was indeed at hand. This summer an election was to be held in Kentucky; there was only one real issue before the State: union or secession. The president of the Bridge Company, John W. Finnell, was a candidate for the State Legislature. Personally a very popular man, he tried at first during the campaign to keep this issue in the background. He was a pro-Union man, but he disliked the Lincoln Administration and its policies.

When the Chicago and Cincinnati Airline Railroad was opened at the end of July, S. S. L'Hommedieu invited the Covington City Council, Finnell, and a few others to be his guests on an excursion to the Windy City. When the men returned the next week, they were enthusiastic about Chicago. The sight of this energetic new city on Lake Michigan, and the strength of the Union sentiment in Covington gradually induced Finnell to come out openly on a strong Union platform.

The campaign closed early in August, and the election was held. When the returns were made known, John Finnell and Green Clay Smith, the Union candidates, had defeated Stevenson and Rankin, secessionists, for the State Legislature. In September, Finnell and Smith, now members-elect from Kenton County, left Covington for Frankfort to assume their legislative duties. Thus the president of the Bridge Company was called away from private business by public responsibilities.

A few days later Colonel Finnell was to pay for his loyalties. As the Cincinnati *Commercial* carried the story, "The barn and stable on Colonel Finnell's farm, near Canton, was destroyed by fire a few nights ago, and a quantity of harness was cut to pieces, which was found in an adjoining outhouse. . . ." As this and similar outrages were committed on the property of Union men, the newspaper reported the general belief that they were attempts at political retaliation.

With the president of the company away and Shinkle busy with the Home Guards, activities were necessarily suspended for some time. Before many weeks had passed, almost all of the bridge directors were occupied with other work.

One Saturday night in the latter part of September, a company of eight or ten men rode up to Moffatt's farmhouse, about fifteen miles south of Covington on the Bank Lick and Independence Turnpike. The captain introduced himself to Moffatt as Amos Shinkle, and said he and a detachment of his men had come out to guard bridges on the Kentucky Central Railroad. There was an attack to be made on the railroad soon, the captain said, and if necessary arms were not secured to defend it, it might be demolished. Other Union men had already handed over their arms, and he would be much obliged if Moffatt would do likewise. Moffatt returned to his house, and in a few minutes he and his boys returned with their guns—loaded. They were ready to give their visitors a good hearty reception; but the ingenious scoundrel who tried to impersonate Shinkle was nowhere to be found.

Before long the Government called again on Shinkle for assistance. The war in the West required extensive movement of men and materials, and the railroads in existence at the time were unable to meet the demands. Shinkle, who was still primarily a coal dealer, owned three boats, however, which could be of great value in transporting soldiers and supplies down the Ohio. For a considerable period these boats were taken over to meet the needs of the army. Before the end of the first year, Shinkle's coal office at the corner of Fourth and Scott Streets was taken over for a recruiting station by Lieutenant E. G. Holden.

During October, Adjutant General Scott Brown resigned from his office, and Governor Magoffin appointed John Finnell to take his place. The Shinkle home was now turned into an office of the Ladies' Soldiers' Relief Society, and there the women of Covington met to take care of sewing soldiers' clothing. Mrs. Amos Shinkle was treasurer of the sewing circle, and one of its most effective managers.

About the same time, it seemed as though Covington might be in need of direct protection. With Amos Shinkle in charge of the work, embankments were thrown up on the hills overlooking the city. The work started in the neighborhood of the "first tunnel" on the Kentucky Central Railroad toward the end of September. By October second the earthworks were completed and ready for the reception of siege guns. Fortunately it was never necessary to use them; but the precaution was not altogether idle.

At the end of the year, a serious problem of caring for the needy developed rather quickly.

Instead of a war boom, a war depression came into being; and this added to the problem left as men left their families to volunteer for service in the army. Early in December, therefore, Shinkle and William Ernst, the president of Covington City Council and one of the Board of Directors of the Bridge Company, called a public meeting to devise measures for the relief of the poor. At the meeting, which was held at Union Hall, Shinkle was chairman and Ernst was the chief speaker. Several hundred dollars in cash and pledges of two hundred bushels of corn were received, and a committee—which again included members of the Bridge Company Board of Directors—was appointed to take further action. Before the end of the month, a soup house had been opened where meals were given, and direct relief, such as fuel, clothing, and food was distributed.

While Shinkle, as one of the prominent citizens of Covington, was in the midst of this work, the other men associated with the Bridge Company likewise found that the responsibilities of the war left little spare time. No wonder then, during the first year of the war, that the Bridge Company was inactive. Its directors were far more active than ever before in the great issue the nation was trying to solve.

SIEGE OF CINCINNATI

DURING the first year of the war, the Confederacy did rather well. There were setbacks in the West, in Missouri, and West Virginia. But the chief campaign of 1861 had ended in Northern defeat at the First Battle of Bull Run.

The next spring, 1862, the Northern command changed, and a new strategy was adopted. By the beginning of June the Union armies were within sight of the Confederate capital, Richmond. In the West, things went even harder for the Confederates this year. Starting early in February, General Grant shoved his way up the Tennessee and Cumberland Rivers, taking Nashville, the capital of Tennessee, and then Corinth, Mississippi, one of the most important railway centers in the South. As a result of the loss of Corinth, the Confederates had to give up Memphis. New Orleans was captured for the Union by Admiral Farragut in April. The spring thus saw the Confederates losing three of their great cities, Nashville, Memphis, and New Orleans, and a large part of Western territory.

It seemed as though a desperate rally would be needed to save their Western position. Acting on this belief, early in July Colonel John Morgan made a sudden dash from Tennessee into Kentucky. At Tompkinsville he surprised a small body of Pennsylvania cavalry, and then advanced, with cavalry and infantry, to Glasgow, Barren County, Kentucky. The following day he issued a proclamation to the people of Kentucky, calling on them to join the Confederacy.

The same afternoon, Saturday, July twelfth, Adjutant General Finnell wired this information to Captain Shinkle and William Ernst in Covington. Those two men at once called a meeting of citizens to assemble at the armory at eight o'clock that evening. There it was their intention to organize the Home Guard Companies and take such other steps as would place Covington in a complete state of defense.

By evening, the additional information wired by Finnell completely changed their plans. When the meeting opened, Shinkle, Ernst, and others presented the latest information they had received. Volunteers were needed to go to Lexington, for that was Morgan's objective. Who was ready to go? About one hundred and eighty men stepped forward and gave their names, foremost among them Captain Shinkle himself. They left for Lexington on a special train, half an hour after midnight.

An hour and a half later, at two o'clock Sunday morning, a detachment of the Fifty-second Ohio Infantry, two hundred and forty strong, followed on another train; and at four o'clock in the morning two hundred and eighty more left for Lexington. Sunday evening, the Ohio Eighty-fifth Regiment and two companies of the Ohio Eighty-eighth followed.

News of the raid threw Covington into great excitement, and all day Sunday nothing else was thought of but defense. When Monday's newspapers appeared, bold-face type and a full column of news and rumors of his raid testified to its importance. The same papers carried word from Louisville that the train from Nashville was more than six hours late. Passengers reported that Morgan had passed within seven miles of Cave City, and had left there with fifteen hundred men for Lexington. The next day Morgan was reported to have been at Versailles, county seat of Wood County. It was a perfect location from which to threaten the entire Bluegrass.

At three o'clock Tuesday afternoon Morgan was at Midway, only fourteen miles from Lexington and fifteen miles from Frankfort on the Louisville and Lexington Railway. The telegraph was cut there, bridges burned, and the railroad torn up. Morgan was reported going to Cynthiana or Paris by way of Georgetown. Thanks to the speed and energy with which troops had been collected for the defense of Lexington, there was no danger of his attacking either that city or Frankfort.

On Wednesday, Morgan captured Georgetown. Later the same afternoon he surrounded Paris, the second town north of Lexington, and demanded its surrender. As the city was held by three hundred and fifty Federal troops, the demand was refused, and Morgan moved on.

Thursday evening he reached Cynthiana, north of Paris, and the last considerable town before Covington. A battle began here about five o'clock. Covington remained in constant communication with Cynthiana—then, suddenly, the wires went dead. Morgan's men had cut the line. Covington was thrown into a panic. The battle lasted only about thirty minutes, when Morgan took the city and sacked it.

With Lexington to the south still in Union hands, Morgan dared not travel any farther north, in spite of this victory. As he turned south, the wires were repaired, and on Friday morning the results of the battle were telegraphed to Covington. That evening, as a result of the fall of Cynthiana, Paris was evacuated by the Union forces; and the same evening at six, Covington was placed under martial law.

Yet the worst of the danger was already over. Without Lexington, Morgan's position was hopeless; and Lexington was too securely held. Within a few days the counterattack was on Morgan's trail, and before the end of the month the raid was ended. Morgan escaped into Tennessee.

Morgan's first raid had failed; his forces were too small to meet the situation, and he had received almost no support either from his own army or from the citizens of Kentucky. But the needs of the South were still acute, and the brilliant raider had shown that something could be done to retrieve the situation in the West.

During August, 1862, another expedition was formed by the Confederate leaders, this time on a much greater scale. Braxton Bragg and Kirby Smith were given an army with which to invade Kentucky, reach the Ohio, seize Cincinnati, and cut the Baltimore and Ohio Railroad. With ten times as many men as Morgan had with him, Kirby Smith moved into Kentucky, and on September first captured Lexington.

Morgan's raid was but child's play compared to this. Here was a danger which required every effort of the community. Under General Lew Wallace, Cincinnati was placed in a state of defense, with the slogan "Citizens for defense, soldiers for battle." All business was suspended, martial law went into effect, and rich and poor alike helped to fortify the Kentucky hills, assemble supplies, and prepare in other ways for a state of siege.

Meanwhile, at Governor Tod's call, soldiers from all over Ohio were hurrying to Cincinnati, to share in defending the city against imminent attack. Now more than ever before, on both sides of the river, men realized the necessity of having ready access from one shore to the other. Boats could not begin to handle the burden placed on them. Men by the thousands had to be taken to Kentucky, and without delay.

To meet this great necessity, a pontoon bridge

Showing both bridge towers unfinished, and man in foreground of procession carrying umbrella

was constructed from Cincinnati to Covington, the first bridge here across the Ohio. Across this unprotected board road the picturesque "squirrel hunters" and "Zouaves" walked—out of step, lest the bridge be destroyed—over to the Kentucky shore. Covington could not be permitted to fall to Kirby Smith; and there was no other way of moving enough soldiers and supplies across the river to protect it.

The siege of Cincinnati was averted. Kirby Smith did not approach the city. But the seriousness of the danger at last woke Cincinnati to the need for a bridge. Not the return of quiet and confidence, but the intensity of the crisis was responsible for the next change which came in the fortunes of the Bridge Company.

In May, 1862, President Finnell had tendered his resignation. "Other duties, public and private, demand all my time and energies," he explained. At that time, about $132,000 had been subscribed to the new stock, and the company was so far encouraged that they said, "It is thought that work will be recommenced during the summer." After the first year of war, some of the citizens were aware of the great need for a bridge.

But after the September "siege" of Cincinnati, events moved faster than ever before. During November, the work of securing additional preferred stock subscription proceeded rapidly and smoothly. At the December meeting of the board, a committee was appointed to procure an amendment to the charter, so as to lower the center of the bridge twenty-two feet.

John Roebling perhaps best described the change which occurred in these words: "When the whole power of the nation was absorbed in its struggle with that gigantic Southern rebellion, fresh endeavors were made by the friends of the work, in conjunction with some prominent capitalists on the Cincinnati side, to resuscitate their sleeping enterprise. The great exigencies of the war, by the movement of troops and materials across the river, made the want of a permanent bridge all the more felt. It is a fact, worthy of historical notice, that in the midst of a general national gloom and despondency, men could be found, with unshaken moral courage and implicit trust in the future political integrity of the nation, willing to risk their capital in the prosecution of an enterprise which usually will only meet support in times of profound peace and general prosperity."

AT WORK AGAIN

FROM the very beginning of January, 1863, there was great activity around the office of the Bridge Company. Two boatloads of stone were ordered for delivery at the Covington tower; and advertisements were made for bids to supply stone, brick, timber, iron, and cement. The president, Jesse Wilcox, began getting in touch with the old contractors, and of course with Roebling. On January nineteenth, after several years' absence, Roebling was once again in Covington, looking things over.

The one change in the bridge which Roebling considered vital now to the complete success of the project was the lowering of the elevation. This had been fixed by legislative enactment at one hundred and twenty-two feet above low water. At such an elevation, with the specified limits on the bridge approaches, the entrances to the bridge would be impossibly steep. Roebling insisted that one hundred feet above low water was the maximum which could be agreed to.

Kentucky passed the desired amendment lowering the elevation early in January, and it was soon brought before the Ohio Legislature for its approval. A powerful and well-organized opposition in Columbus now made its appearance, and for week after week the bridge directors found their request denied.

"The action of the Legislature was so uncertain and doubtful," President Wilcox reported, "that the directors deemed it unsafe to commence work until it was determined."

All other preparations were temporarily suspended while effort was concentrated on this problem. The Cincinnati City Council created a special committee to investigate the question, and published an eight-page *Report* on it which was given wide circulation. The gist of the report was contained in a resolution adopted by the council. The local representatives in the State Legislature were asked to assist in securing the amendment, because it would facilitate intercourse between the two cities by securing an easier grade of entrance and exit to the bridge.

At length, on the last day of March, the Ohio Legislature passed the amendment. The span of the bridge was reduced from fourteen hundred to one thousand feet, and the height to not less than one hundred feet. With this guarantee, the company could now proceed with its plans.

As soon as it was definitely assured that the amendment would be passed, the engineer began to examine the towers. The masonry on the Cincinnati side had been subjected to overflows, and the top course had to resist the action of drift, of steamers, barges, and heavily loaded boats. On resuming operations, the excellence and strength of the masonry of both towers was proved by its unimpaired condition. Not a joint had washed out, and the top course presented a smooth, even floor.

A committee was next appointed to look at the machinery and tools, and have them put in order for use. A great portion of the machinery to be used had already been ordered and made in 1857; but it had never been put into service, and when work was stopped, it was stored away.

The engines and hoisting machinery which were in use in 1856 and 1857 had to be renewed and rebuilt; and this amounted in effect to an entirely new beginning. Shops had to be erected and stocked with new sets of tools. New contracts had to be made with various parties for the delivery of stone and cement; and these too required special consideration.

On resuming work in 1863, Roebling discovered that no satisfactory arrangement could be made for carrying on the work by contract, as had been done in 1856. It was therefore decided to lay the masonry by the day, under the direct supervision of the engineer and his assistants.

"The company has reason to be satisfied with this course, which was indeed the only one left to pursue," Roebling declared. "The masonry has, in my opinion, cost less than it would have cost had the laying been done by contract. No contractors made acceptable offers, because none had experience in such work, to carry up heavy masonry to such a great height. We were therefore obliged to put up all the requisite machinery for hoisting and laying ourselves, but this once done, the rest was easy to accomplish. Instead of paying large profits to the contractors, and transferring the responsibility of the work to other hands, we concluded on doing the laying by the day. The stone cutting was of course done by contract, or by the foot, and all the materials delivered by contract."

The stone cutting on the Cincinnati side was supervised by Mr. Adam Hoplar, and by Mr. Charles Ware on the Covington side. The carpenter work was superintended by Mr. E. F. Farrington; the wire shop was in charge of Mr. D. S. Rhule; and the machine and blacksmith shops in charge of Mr. William Apperly. As superintendents of masonry, seven men served at various times in 1863 and thereafter, and on various portions of the work: John Knox, A. Gilmore, Charles Gillespie, A. H. Acken, George Tudd, John Bell, and John Maloy.

Early in May, the Bridge Company was ready to begin work, and the first call for money was made on the new subscriptions of preferred stock. At the same time Assistant Engineer A. G. Gower arrived in Covington. Within the next few days he closed a number of heavy contracts for stone, iron, cement, timber, and machinery; and soon he had a force of hands at work on the Cincinnati side. Their first task was to prepare the foundations for the engines which were to be used in hoisting stone and cement to the top of the piers. Before the end of May, Roebling too was back in Cincinnati, directing the work which was now under way.

The new plan for building the towers was quite different from the system used in 1856. Roebling himself had worked it out, and described it in the published *Report for 1867*. On this plan all the materials were raised by means of a wire rope of one and one-half inches diameter, winding upon a cast-iron drum of three feet diameter. The rope wound in spiral grooves to save wear. Parallel to the masonry, a strong vertical framework was erected for the support of the hoisting sheave, tracks, and trucks. Each block of stone thus rapidly raised was placed upon a truck and run either right or left to one of the two setting derricks. The derricks were balanced by traversing weights, and so constructed that they were absolutely safe, no matter how high they rose.

The frame of such a derrick consisted of a sound white oak log, twenty inches in diameter and thirty-eight feet long. This log served as a mast, with two booms attached about twenty feet from the lower end. Half way down from this point two cast-iron turntables, six feet in diameter, supported by and revolving on cones, encompassed the mast. This allowed for an easy circular motion around the center. The lower end of the mast served as a tail, confined in a well hole which was left open in the masonry.

With work on the towers progressing so rapidly, Roebling next turned his attention to the anchor pits and piers. On the last of May, the contract for excavating the anchor pits for the bridge on the Covington side was awarded to Mr. T. Woods. On the first of June he was on hand with a large force, ready to begin work.

At about the same time, a bid was accepted from the Niles Works of Cincinnati for the anchor plates. These were the enormous iron cones to be fixed in the anchor piers, and to which the cables were to be attached. Roebling, in urging the acceptance of this bid, wrote, "From the fact that the latter firm have an air furnace in which to prepare the metal for molding and the advantage of delivery . . . in the opinion of your engineer is an advantage that cannot be lightly estimated or scarcely too highly appreciated, for improving the quality and uniformity of the material . . ."

The laying of the masonry on the Cincinnati tower began about the first of July. Within a week, the derricks broke down; and around the fourteenth Roebling wrote, "I have today got through with the reconstruction & erection of my derricks & would commence laying masonry, if martial law had not been declared on account of Morgan's raid . . ."

Notwithstanding various other interruptions, the Cincinnati tower was doubled in height by the end of the season. When work was finally suspended because of cold weather, it rose ninety feet above low water mark.

During July, August, and September, cribbing work was built on the north side of the Covington tower, to protect the foundation and prevent the current from undermining the pier. This cribbing extended fifty feet into the river, and was one hundred feet long.

Both anchor pits were completely excavated during the summer, involving a removal of some eighty-five hundred cubic yards of earth. During the fall, the work of refilling the pits with masonry was commenced, and down to the end of November progressed rapidly. About half as much masonry was laid for the anchors as for the towers during this season.

The activity of the Bridge Company was reflected in many ways, all indicating that at last there was general confidence the bridge would be completed. By the middle of January the bridge was becoming the general topic of conversation. Many were still skeptical of its completion; but on the last day of the month, the *Commercial* reporter wrote: "There is a considerable excitement in real estate in Covington, and sales, during the past two or three weeks, have been large. Prices, of course, are going up. The prospect of the early completion of the Covington and Cincinnati Bridge, and the mania for making investments, caused by the general derangement in the currency of the country, have produced this unexampled stir in property."

A week later the clerk of Kenton County Court reported the number of deeds for property recorded during the preceding two weeks in Covington was fifty per cent greater than the number recorded in Cincinnati during the same period.

With all the preparations going on through

the spring, "Never within the memory of the oldest inhabitant has there been such great activity in real estate in Covington as exists at the present time," the *Commercial* reported at the end of May. "As there is no longer any doubt about the early completion of the Covington and Cincinnati Bridge, we anticipate a still greater demand for building lots." Covington, which at this time had about sixteen thousand people, showed an increase of ten per cent in population in a single year. Considering the numbers who had left to join the army, it was looked on as "a pretty fair increase."

During the early part of July the city heard the usual reports of Morgan's forces, but they were "considered the mere fancies of excited people."

Suddenly, a year to the day after his first appearance, Morgan broke into the local newspapers with a full column of reports. His men had seized a boat, the *Alice Dean,* at Brandenburg, Kentucky, and five thousand of them had crossed over to Indiana. There they took Corydon, Salem, Vernon, and Versailles, and were marching rapidly toward Cincinnati.

Sunday evening all navigation was stopped on the Ohio; and on Monday morning, July thirteenth, General Burnside proclaimed martial law. The people of the river cities once again grew alarmed. After their experiences during the summer before, they were familiar with military rule; but never before had the enemy come so

THE OHIO BRIDGE

close to the city. That very morning, Morgan's force was already moving from Indiana into Ohio, at Harrison.

All business was suspended. Though the derricks at the bridge towers demanded repair, work was brought to a halt while the military resources of the city were mobilized. In Covington on Monday morning all persons subject to military duty were ordered to report to enroll and organize into military companies for the protection of the city. Commissioners, among them Amos Shinkle and Jesse Wilcox, were appointed to enroll and organize the men. Early in the afternoon the commissioners met in the mayor's office, where Colonel Shinkle (a colonel since the time of Kirby Smith's raid in 1862) appointed staff and field officers.

Once again Morgan, though he had more men than before, had fewer than he needed. Cincinnati was the prize he wished to take, but it was too big a prize. He dared not even attack it.

On Tuesday and Wednesday, Morgan's forces divided. One group passed through Springdale and Reading to Miamiville, the other traveled from Glendale to Loveland. They pillaged farms, stole horses, and tore up what they could of the Little Miami Railroad. Then they realized their problem was how to escape.

Martial law came to an end in the river cities Thursday morning. This interruption to work was at an end; and ten days later Morgan was finally captured in eastern Ohio, after a flight of hairbreadth escapes. But there were other difficulties. No sooner was Morgan out of the way than labor troubles began for the Bridge Company, and Roebling was faced with a strike among his workmen. This too was eventually straightened out, and during the fall construction proceeded much more smoothly.

The changes which had come over the Bridge Company in twenty months were almost unbelievable. A company which was almost bankrupt, just able to keep its property and franchise, had suddenly become the chief public work in the city. The Cincinnati tower, which appeared but a useless pile of sandstone, had grown to a height of ninety feet, up to the level where the bridge floor was to be built. The Covington tower lacked but ten feet of this standard. The anchor piers, where the great cables would be fastened, were already taking shape.

BUILDING THE BRIDGE: 1864

IN THE spring of 1864 the Bridge Company was faced with a new financial problem. All prices were rising steadily, but the price of gold was rising at an alarming rate. About half of the $500,000 of preferred stock was already spent by March first, and the rest would be gone in another nine months. In addition to the money which would be needed to carry on the work, the company wished to retire the $25,000 bonds which had been issued in 1861 to contractors and other creditors.

A committee appointed to study the problem recommended in June the adoption of a broadly planned financial program. "Prudence would seem to dictate to your committee," they said, "that it is better in the present financial condition of our country to create a debt on long time at a low rate of interest, which debt will mature when we may certainly expect that specie payment will have been resumed all over the land, and for a sufficient length of time, to admit of but little if any difference between the value of specie and any paper currency which may then exist, than to create a debt at a high rate of interest to mature within the next five to fifteen years, during which time it may be regarded as probable that the transition from the present currency of the country to a coin currency will occur, and during which time, should specie payment be resumed, coin will undoubtedly command a very high premium."

In line with this policy, the board determined to borrow the money required for the completion of the work at a low rate. They proposed thirty-year bonds at six per cent, which they believed could be sold in New York and elsewhere at par as fast as the company needed the money. Since New York, Boston, and Philadelphia represented the cheapest capital in the country, agents were sent to those cities to put the bonds on the market. Altogether, $500,000 of thirty-year bonds were to be issued.

The high value of gold in relation to paper money was a serious difficulty in another way. Roebling was in the market for wire for the bridge cables; but there was not a manufacturer in America who could supply the wire according to the specifications and on the terms the Bridge Company needed it. It was necessary to turn to England to find what was wanted. During the winter, Roebling was in communication with Richard Johnson & Brothers, of Manchester, on the subject. A contract was at last drawn up and sent to the English manufacturers early in March, and accepted by them early in April. Payment for the wire, however, had to be made in coin, not paper money, and here the Bridge Company was at a great disadvantage. But there was no way of avoiding the necessity. Every inch of wire in the original bridge cables was brought three thousand miles and more.

Continued high water in the spring of 1864 delayed the resumption of work for some weeks; but the work of laying stone on the Covington pier was begun Monday, May 9. At the same time a large force was put to work on the anchor pits there. The stone work done on the bridge this summer comprised three parts: anchor piers, cable piers or towers, and abutments.

The anchor piers were built of limestone bases, and finished with light-colored freestone brought chiefly from the Buena Vista quarries near Portsmouth, Ohio. The foundations were nearly thirty feet below the grade of Water Street, Cincinnati, and Front Street, Covington. The piers in Covington measured sixty by ninety feet on the ground; those in Cincinnati, sixty by one hundred feet.

Embedded in these piers were the enormous cast-iron anchor plates to which the cables were attached. During the summer and fall the anchor chains were forged in the shops of the Bridge Company. By the end of the season, seven links of the anchor chain on the Cincinnati side were completed, and six links on the Covington side were likewise completed and in place. Forty-five more bars were on hand, and one hundred and thirty more were wanted. These the company expected to manufacture in their own blacksmith shop during the coming winter.

As the towers had now reached a height of more than ninety feet, the construction was modified to provide an arch through which the roadway would pass. A different method was also used in raising the stone above this level. Much poplar lumber was used in carrying up the stone work of the towers. Four heavy frames some six feet wide were used, extending from the floor of the bridge to the top of the stonework. These frames supported a railway reaching across the front part of the towers. On this two little trucks were placed, on wheels, to receive the stones as they were hoisted and carry them to the derricks on either side of the towers, as they might be required. Enclosed between two of these frames were a series of wooden ladders by which workmen ascended to the top of the towers. In the evening, when there were few observers, adventurous visitors climbed up these ladders to test their nerves.

During this entire season the scarcity of mechanics, stone cutters, stone masons, and setters was a serious drawback in the progress of the work. The requirements of the army in the conduct of war had taken away a large proportion of skilled workmen; and more than once Roebling found construction going slower than anticipated, because of the lack of an efficient force.

The early part of December was extremely cold this year, much colder than usual. The Bridge Company had to suspend operations about three weeks earlier than the previous season. Thus again the work had not progressed so far as they had hoped.

While the piers and anchorages were not ready for the cables at the end of 1864, work on them had come along very well. When the *Annual Report* was drawn up in the winter, the directors confidently expected that work on the cables would be started by the end of the following spring.

1865: FIRST YEAR OF PEACE

THE Civil War was now drawing to an end, and the whole country was encouraged by the prospect of an early peace. Since November, 1864, it was evident that the Confederate Government could not survive many months. In April it finally collapsed. With the end of this great military conflict a new era was opened in the history of the nation.

During the winter, the Board of Directors came to the conclusion that the bridge should be "Nationalized." Instead of being entirely a private structure, it should be declared a lawful structure for the purpose of transmitting the mails of the United States over it, to and from the various States in the line of its route.

Accordingly in January one of the directors, Theodore Cook, was appointed a committee to visit Congress for the purpose of having such a bill enacted. Early in March he returned to Cincinnati, reporting the passage by both houses of Congress of the measure desired:

"To establish a bridge across the Ohio River at Cincinnati a post road. Be it enacted by the Senate and the House of Representatives of the United States of America in Congress assembled, That the bridge across the Ohio River at Cincinnati, in the State of Ohio, and at Covington, in the State of Kentucky, is hereby declared to be, when completed, in accordance with the laws of the States of Kentucky and Ohio, a lawful structure and post road for the conveyance of the mails of the United States."

The financial problem of the year before was taken care of by the final payments on preferred stock subscriptions. This year, it was met with an additional stock issue.

Early in January, the board resolved to apply to the Ohio and Kentucky Legislatures for an amendment to the charter authorizing the issue of $250,000 additional preferred stock. The amendment was passed by Kentucky on January twenty-first, increasing the capital stock to $1,250,000 altogether. Ohio passed the act about eight weeks later.

In due time a meeting of stockholders was held, with all but one of the stockholders present voting in favor of accepting the terms of the amended charter. The next day the board announced:

"WHEREAS, The stockholders by a large majority of their vote at a meeting held at the office of the company on the 5th April 1865, decided to increase the capital stock of the company to $1,250,000, of which amount $750,000 is to be preferred stock; therefore,

"*Resolved,* That the president be instructed to open the books for subscriptions to increase the preferred stock to $750,000, said books to be opened at the office of the company in Covington, April 13th, at 3 P. M., and to remain open according to the provisions of the charter until said stock is subscribed, and that he give due notice thereof by advertisement in a newspaper circulating in Covington and Cincinnati."

One week later the entire amount of the new stock had been subscribed, and the stock books were declared to be closed.

In mid-March Roebling informed the board that he was ready for the shipment of wire from England. Richard Johnson & Brothers had been working on the order for very nearly a year, and some sixty tons of the wire were now ready. The order was sent out about the first of April, and the money to pay for the wire was sent along with it. A few weeks later the first consignments began to arrive.

During the whole building season, the minutes of the Board of Directors were taken up with long lists of bills presented and allowed. These, together with the regular calls for money, the redemption and cancellation of old bonds, and some other details of finance made up almost the entire business of the company.

The construction went steadily forward without accidents or hindrances, except those in the spring. Then, as usual, floods interfered with the work. This year, instead of prolonged high water, there were a series of freshets, which submerged machinery in place and drove the men around the tower from their work. The completion of the masonry was thus delayed about six weeks in the early part of the summer.

The character of the work seems even to have affected the dry chronicles of the secretary. On July 13, 1865, he wrote in the minutes, "After a good deal of talk, profitable and unprofitable, and without the transaction of further business, the board adjourned."

THE FOOT BRIDGE

BEFORE the end of September, 1865, the two massive cable piers were finished. Two hundred and thirty feet they rose above the river. From the foundation to the passage for the road, a distance of ninety feet, they were slightly irregular in form, with two offsets. The great portals through the towers were seventy-five feet in height. Just at the spring of the arch over the roadway in each tower was a small opening, reached from the floor by a wire rope ladder. From this opening, stone steps and wooden ladders extended to a scuttle in the roof of the tower. The tops were as yet unfinished.

On either side of each tower stood two huge anchor piers, solid blocks of stone and concrete. In them lay embedded the anchor plates and chains. Between the anchor piers, rising slightly toward the towers, were the abutments. From them the floor of the bridge would spring to the passage through the towers. From the sidewalk on Water Street, Cincinnati, to the floor of the bridge was sixteen feet; the height from the sidewalk on Front Street, Covington, was about twenty feet.

There these great structures stood. From center to center of the towers was a distance of one thousand and fifty-seven feet. But the gap was as yet unbridged. The towers were isolated, like strangers staring at each other.

In September the first wire cables were finished at the Roebling factory in Trenton, New Jersey. The two and one-half inch wire came from the factory in reels. In Cincinnati the reels were mounted on wooden shafts, and then suspended on a frame on Water Street. The free end of the wire rope was first fastened in the anchor pier, and then passed over the short distance to the Cincinnati tower. There it was hoisted to the top of the tower by the same machinery that was used in lifting the stones. Once it was laid in the huge iron saddle at the top of the tower, the rest was coiled in a flatboat on the other side, fitted up with apparatus for playing it out easily and without kinking. The flatboat was then towed across the river to the Covington side, the rope being payed out and sunk to the bottom of the river.

In Covington the rope was hoisted up and passed over the Covington tower. It was then taken back to the south anchor, looped, and started on the return trip across the river.

A powerful tackle, operated by steam, was attached to the rope, and at a time when there was little passing of steamers it was drawn, glistening and dripping out of the water and up to its proper position. The ends were then made fast to the anchor piers.

This wire, called a guide wire, was used to

regulate the next, and all the others which were now stretched over the towers from one anchorage to the other. When these cables were finished, suspenders were attached, composed of nine wires laid in a similar manner. Cross beams were then fastened between each pair of suspenders, oak planks three feet long, and two and one-half by six and one-half inches thick.

An oak flooring was then laid across these beams. Four pieces formed the full width of the floor, about twenty-seven inches. Two oak slats on each side, attached to the suspenders, formed the railings. The planks were secured to the beams by round iron bolts one-half inch in diameter.

Thus the first bridge was built, a miniature suspension bridge, complete in almost every detail.

The foot bridge was first crossed an hour before noon, Wednesday, October 4, from Cincinnati to Covington. It was put up primarily for the convenience of the workmen in carrying on the construction; but before the end of the week hundreds of persons were making applications every day for permission to cross. All were refused, as their crossing would interfere with the operations of the workmen.

In still weather this bridge could be crossed in comparative comfort and safety; but on windy days, steady nerves, quick hands and feet, and some knowledge of navigation were necessary.

The time had now come when thousands of persons regularly came to watch the progress of the work. It was no longer simply a matter of hoisting stones and setting them, but of activity which stretched more than a thousand feet across the water. One old gentleman, looking at the twenty-seven inch foot bridge swinging high over the river, remarked that "after all the talk about a fine bridge, it is a very flimsy affair."

Many amusing stories of this foot bridge are told by E. F. Farrington, the master carpenter of the bridge, who brought out his own account of it when the bridge was opened. Adventurers ambitious to cross the bridge offered many a bribe and excuse to pass the watchmen in charge. Some favored ones were permitted to make the attempt; a few succeeded in crossing, while others retreated in fear and trembling.

Farrington told of a "fair and fat" preacher who essayed the feat on his hands and knees; but after crawling a short distance the flesh gave out and he retired. Another brave fellow from Cincinnati eluded the vigilance of the watchmen with the aid of a heavy fog one morning. He clambered up the wooden ladders then standing at the towers, and started across. But he, too, came to his hands and knees.

Several ladies crossed at different times, and a few ventured to climb the ladders to the top of the towers. Farrington admitted that he had been coaxed into gallanting two young ladies over the bridge, and up on to the Covington tower, one starry night. The damsels behaved bravely, he reported, and made no demonstrations of nervousness beyond a little desperate hugging and squealing in the most giddy places.

The bridge now began securing press notices throughout the whole country. The New York *News* was but one of many papers which in October described the wonders of the new structure. In an article on "The Great Cincinnati Bridge," it was compared with other suspension bridges then in existence. More than two hundred feet longer than the suspension bridge over the Niagara River, and more than five hundred and fifty feet longer than the Menai Bridge in England, it would be the longest in the world.

Three times the foot bridge was badly broken by high winds. Once it was pulled apart for a distance of twelve feet near the Cincinnati tower. The last time, the whole stationery portion through the Covington tower was thrown into the river.

As soon as the foot bridge was completed, the work of manufacturing permanent cables was commenced. By November 7 the stretching of the wires for the great cables was begun. It was expected to take about six months to construct the cables. The foot bridge remained until the main floor beams were suspended, and then it was removed.

Neither high water nor cold weather could stop the work now. Only one year's further work was needed to complete the bridge. With the goal in sight, every energy was directed toward pushing the work.

Wrapping the Cables

THE BRIDGE COMPLETED

THREE great steps in the building of the bridge were now finished. The cable piers had been built. The anchor piers, too, were completed, with the enormous anchor plates and chains in them. And the river had been bridged by a slender pathway suspended from thin wire ropes far above the river.

But the great superstructure of the suspension bridge had still to be created. The highway across the river was not yet in existence.

During the early part of January, 1866, the weather was mild and favorable to the continuation of work. Three-fourths of the wire for the cables had been received from England, and most of it was prepared. This preparation consisted first of oiling with three coats of linseed oil, to keep it from rusting. Then the wire was spliced. This was done by flattening the ends of two coils, lapping them together, and wrapping them with small enameled wire. The splices were thus made as strong as the original wire itself.

Work in the various shops of the company was being pushed forward with vigor. As the wire was prepared, it was taken to the anchorage, fastened, and passed over the first cable tower. It was then taken across the river and passed over a pulley on the opposite tower, where a hundred-pound weight was attached to bring it up to the proper position.

After the first wire was taken across, great progress was made. The average number of wires taken across daily was about eighty. They were carried on spider-like wheels, which ran constantly back and forth. Beginning in November, 1865, they kept steadily at work, through heat and cold, stopping only at night or when winds sweeping up the river made it impossible to continue.

The wires numbered fifty-two hundred, and the two great cables were to be composed of seven strands each. The fourth strand of the first cable was completed in January, and work went on with very little interruption. As soon as one strand was completed it was wrapped and lowered into its place immediately, and work started on the next. By the middle of April, the fourth strand of the second cable was completed. There remained but three strands to be made, and with anything like fair weather the engineers expected to finish them in three months. The bridge would be ready for foot passengers, according to that estimate, before the end of the year.

Toward the end of May a severe windstorm struck the cities. The foot bridge was broken near the Covington tower, but fortunately the damage could be repaired in a few hours.

By the beginning of June, the sixth strand was completed and lowered to its place, and work started on the seventh and last. The little wheels carrying the wires across the river moved ceaselessly to and fro, crossing a thousand times, two thousand times, five thousand times.

At 11.10 on the morning of June 23, the last wire was run over. The wheels had crossed the river ten thousand three hundred and sixty times, carrying five thousand, one hundred and eighty wires across the river and back. The last of the fourteen strands for the cables was wrapped and lowered; and as an observer wrote, "Much pleasure was felt by all concerned in the progress of the work on the completion of this the most important and tedious part of it."

The wrapping of the cables was begun immediately. The wires, which were laid straight, not twisted, were compressed and wrapped around closely with one thickness of galvanized iron wire. Iron clamps, with bolts and nuts, were used for this purpose. About twenty or twenty-five feet per day was the average progress in wrapping, which was done by an ingenious machine called a "spider." Through the entire process, the wire was kept saturated with linseed oil and Spanish brown, and then given a final coat of white lead and oil.

For wrapping and for other purposes where it was necessary for workmen to leave the ground, traveling scaffolds suspended from the cables were used. These were attached to iron shrieves which rested on the cables, and could be moved along them to suit convenience. The first small wire rope, which still remained suspended above the cables, was used as a guide rope by the workmen, to steady themselves as they walked up and down on the cables.

The wrapping of the two great cables was finished in the early part of August, and a large number of workmen were soon engaged in fastening the suspenders. Flat-iron bands, cut to encircle the cables, were first made in the company's shop in Cincinnati. Taken to the scene of operations, they were heated in a portable forge, placed on the foot bridge, and opened so as to slip easily over the cable.

In this condition they were passed up at a dark red heat to the men on the staging, who shrunk them and fitted them around the wires. The suspenders were then attached to these straps by sockets and bolts, and allowed to hang down in readiness to receive the floor beams.

The bands and suspenders were fastened to the cables at intervals of five feet on each side. Altogether there were three hundred and three pairs. By the end of August, with these suspenders hanging in place, the structure began to look "very much like a bridge indeed."

In the meantime, the wrought-iron floor beams had been received from a factory in Buffalo, New York. They were between six and seven hundred in number, and nineteen and one-half feet in length. During the winter, spring, and summer workmen in the Bridge Company shops were busy splicing them, making beams thirty-nine feet long,

CINCINNATI AND COVINGTON
SUSPENSION BRIDGE.

THE CABLES COMPLETED

the width of the bridge. The work of laying these wrought-iron joists was begun toward the end of August, and finished shortly after the last suspenders were made ready for them. By the early part of September the three hundred and three suspended floor beams, and twenty beams through the towers, which had no connection with the cables, were ready for the floor.

A planing mill had been erected by the company on the wharf on the Covington side. There the joists for the flooring were jointed and brought to a uniform thickness during the summer, and a drying house for seasoning the timber was in operation.

During September, the workmen were crossing the permanent bridgeway on rough planking. The work remaining to be done consisted of adjusting the girders beneath the beams the length of the bridge, laying the flooring, adjusting the trusses and railing, and completing the ornamentation of the towers.

Some six hundred thousand feet of oak and pine lumber were consumed in making the floor. The full thickness of the floor in the original carriage way was seven and one-half inches, in three thicknesses. All were of kiln-dried oak. The middle floor was soaked in coal tar, and the two upper floors were laid in a mixture of coal tar and rosin. Nearly three hundred barrels of tar were used in the construction of the bridge. The under floor of the sidewalk was made of white pine, and the top floor of oak.

The under floor was fastened to the iron beams by bolts and nuts, and the top floors were fastened with wooden screws, to avoid rusting out.

The approaches to the bridge were paved during November with blocks of seasoned oak, known as "Nicholson pavement." Stone flagging, nine feet wide, was laid on either side of the carriage way in Covington.

With the construction of the bridge in the last stages, the directors turned their attention to other matters which had not been considered before. A schedule had to be drawn up, tickets printed, and agents, collectors, and watchmen employed.

On the last Saturday in November, 1866, President Shinkle announced that the bridge would be opened one week later, Saturday, December 1. Tickets were placed on sale, and during the ensuing week the newspapers were filled with accounts of the great bridge, the longest in the world.

OPENING DAY

THE last few days in November were cold and unpleasant, with light drizzling rains and temperatures about freezing. On the very last day the rain stopped, but the sky was still cloudy.

Saturday morning, the first of December, was clear and mild. At sunrise, a gun squad from the Newport Barracks fired a salute of one hundred guns with two brass twelve-pounders at the foot of Greenup Street, in salute to the opening of the bridge. From the first hour on, there was a mighty rush of people. Up the unfinished approaches they swarmed, men, women, and children, excited by curiosity to avail themselves of the first opportunity to cross the great bridge.

By noon the mercury registered forty degrees. It seemed as though the entire population of Covington, Cincinnati, and Newport had turned out for an over-the-water promenade. Newspapers advised all promenaders "to go very warmly clad, as it is very cold out there, over the water, with a keenly cutting wintry wind whistling along the river. The change experienced in the atmosphere in passing from the shore to the middle of the bridge is like that felt when one leaves a partially warmed room for the unprotected street, on a New Year's day, for instance." By sunset, the number who had crossed was forty-six thousand.

The following day, Sunday, was more pleasant. It was clear, and another rise brought the noonday temperature to fifty. Eight or ten men were busy all day long on the Covington side, selling tickets and taking them up, while on the Cincinnati side fourteen men were at work. Yet at three o'clock the crowd was so great at the Cincinnati end that people had to wait in long lines before being able to get their tickets.

The residents of Covington were amazed at the hordes which descended on them. "The beautiful weather and the attraction of the great bridge," wrote the reporter, "brought out thousands upon thousands, the most of them from Cincinnati, and on some of the principal thoroughfares and sidewalks it was so densely crowded that locomotion was difficult." By the evening of the second day, an additional one hundred and twenty thousand persons had crossed the bridge. From morning 'til night, the bridge was literally black with pedestrians. "It is the great attractive feature of the city."

The footway floorings were as yet uncompleted, so that the foot passengers had to use one of the roadways intended for vehicles. The gas light fixtures and the heavy iron trusses separating the roadways from the footways were likewise unfinished. Nor were the turrets cov-

Published by F. Mendenhall Cincinnati.

CINCINNATI & COVINGTON SUSPENSION BRIDGE

THE BRIDGE IN 1867

ering the saddles at the tops of the cable piers built to their full thirty-foot height.

During the rest of December, further work was done toward completing the bridge. The brick turrents (later to be removed) were added to the towers; the iron trusses separating the roadways from the footways were completed; and the footway floorings and the ornamental iron railings giving protection on the water sides were constructed. Work was done, too, on the approaches to the bridge.

Now winter descended on the city. On the next to the last day of December, the ice in the river was so heavy that it was with great difficulty the ferry boats could run. Their trips were sometimes an hour apart. The *Cincinnati Belle* and the *Newport Belle* were carried down the river a mile or two by the ice early in the morning, and did not get back to their docks until three o'clock in the afternoon. Of course, all who desired to cross the river during their absence availed themselves of the new bridge.

The last day of the year was cold and hazy. A southwest wind threatened snow, and the river was still full of heavy ice. "Owing to the necessities of the public in consequence of ice in the Ohio River, and the inability of the ferry boats to run, it became necessary to open the bridge for vehicles sooner than was originally intended."

On Tuesday morning, New Year's Day, the newspapers carried this announcement:

"The Covington and Cincinnati Suspension

Bridge will be opened this morning for vehicles of all kinds. The arrangement, it must be understood, is only temporary, as the bridge is not yet completed, and the crossing of vehicles will interfere with the workmen very materially, if it does not put a stop entirely to their operation. The necessity for the opening, however, is apparent. The present condition of the river shows the importance of the bridge: and the managers are doing their best to accommodate the public, even to the detriment of their own interests."

The formal opening of the Covington and Cincinnati Suspension Bridge took place at eleven o'clock in the morning. A procession of carriages and horsemen was formed at the office of the Bridge Company on Greenup Street, Covington. Against the freezing wind it moved across the bridge in the following order:

1. Carriage containing the president of the Bridge Company and the engineer.
2. Carriage containing the vice-president of the Bridge Company and the assistant engineer.
3. Carriages containing the bridge directors.
4. Carriages containing members of the City Council of Covington.
5. Two horsemen.
6. Carriages containing citizens of Covington.

When this procession reached Cincinnati it was joined at the end of the bridge by a much larger procession, composed of the cars of the Adams, American, Harnden, United States, and Mer-

THE OHIO BRIDGE

chants' Union Express Companies, filled with employees of these institutions, and a large number of omnibuses, containing railroad men and others. The processions thus united, marched back over the bridge to the music of Menter's and Heidel's bands, amid the shouts of the thousands who lined both shores of the river. Upon reaching the Covington side, the procession marched through the principal streets, and later returned to Cincinnati.

In the afternoon a large number of carriages and other vehicles crossed the bridge. From all indications, about forty-five or fifty thousand persons crossed the structure on New Year's Day.

That evening, about eleven o'clock, two citizens were returning home from their last "call." As they crossed the bridge, they witnessed the flight of a beautiful meteor across the heavens. It started from near the zenith, coursing in a southeast direction, throwing off such a brilliant light that distinct shadows of the persons were cast on the sidewalks for the space of a minute at least, until the nebulae exploded near the horizon. It left a clear and beautiful streak of light through its whole course that remained visible, and then faded away into misty wavelets, apparently as if moved by a gentle zephyr. "Let none who did not witness this beautiful phenomenon," the reporter added, "say that it was owing to the numerous 'calls' that the gentlemen had made during the day enabled them to see heavenly bodies at night, for they had a witness along."

The estimate placed on the value of the bridge in Roebling's first Annual Report after the bridge was opened contained no hint of mere material values:

"Evening lectures, concerts, and other innocent and rational amusements, for the old as well as for the young, offered in the city of Cincinnati, may now be enjoyed by the denizens of Covington with more facility and ease than can be done by those who reside north of the Queen City. By means of street cars the center of one city may be reached from the center of the other in about fifteen minutes, and at any time during the night. Is not this an improvement upon the old method of ferrying across the river, say nothing of the mud and obstructions by ice in the winter!"

The report of the directors at the same time was perhaps more to the point:

"It is scarcely deemed necessary to say to you that the bridge is a complete success. Perhaps no work of its magnitude has ever been more so, the wonder and admiration of all who cross it, and in the future there will doubtless few visit the city of Cincinnati or its vicinity who will not cross this magnificent structure."

A QUARTER CENTURY OF THE BRIDGE

AMOS SHINKLE entered the Bridge Company in 1856. Ten years later, in large part as a result of his wisdom, energy, and strength, the Ohio Bridge was completed and opened as the greatest bridge in the world. For another quarter of a century Shinkle watched the bridge prosper with America. Through the Civil War, the deepest crisis in the nation's history, he had guarded and fostered it. When that crisis was past, and America returned to the long road upward among nations, he had the pleasure of helping the bridge keep step with her progress.

At first the path was a rough one. Though the bridge was now fully open to traffic, there was much still to be done. The construction itself had not been finished, owing to the urgent necessity for the opening of the bridge.

Final completion still required several months of labor, finishing the sidewalks, ornaments on the tops of the towers, and necessary offices for the use of the company. The railings were finished shortly after the middle of March, and the turrets about the middle of May; the sidewalk planking was also completed in May; and the painting of the cables and the ironwork by the first of June. By July, everything was at last finished.

Other problems were coming up. There were questions of individual and packaged tickets, and trouble with counterfeiters. The bridge masonry offered wonderful opportunities to bill posters, and the directors had before the end of the first year to reach a policy on leasing anchorage and approach walls for advertisements. A contract had to be made with the Covington Street Railway Company covering rates, types of service, and the amount of track to be laid on each side of the river.

Traffic rules had to be adopted, and the first code was issued in February, 1867. It was frequently amended during the first few months, as experience was gained. The principal terms were that foot passengers keep off the roadways, and that all travel keep to the right. Processions of all kinds were required to break step when passing over the bridge; no turning of vehicles was allowed; and live stock had to be divided into lots of not more than twenty-five head of horses, cattle, or mules, one hundred hogs, or one hundred and fifty sheep.

Although the bridge was completed and yielding revenue, there were bills coming due in far larger sums than the income could take care of. Additional loans had to be made, and it was several years before the earnings of the bridge were more than enough to meet current obligations to creditors.

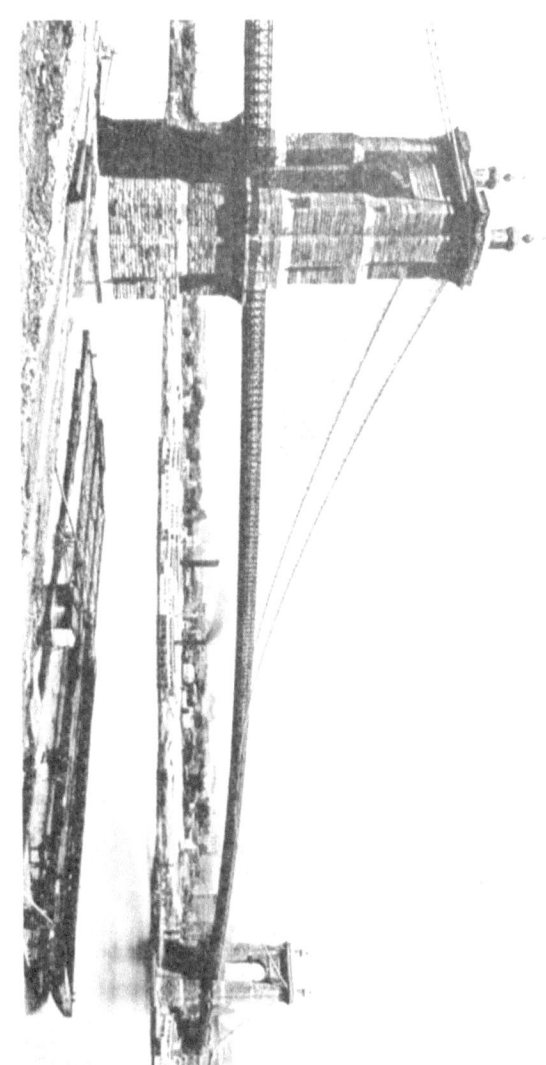

The Old Bridge: 1880

During the 1870's and '80's, the bridge traffic gradually improved, but in the first twenty years it never surpassed the level set in 1871, the fifth year after the opening. Foot passengers formed a large part of the traffic; in 1888, a banner year, about four and one-half million foot crossings were made. Other sources of revenue were found in rents from the telegraph companies, which in 1867 first ran their wires across the bridge; and in similar rents from the telephone company which began interstate service here in 1882. Gradually the loans which the company had made were paid off, and the various bond issues were retired.

Only two years after the bridge was opened, in July, 1869, John Roebling died. The master architect was still striving for even greater achievements in the work which made his name famous. His memory was fittingly honored by the associates with whom he had built the Ohio Bridge:

"The death of John A. Roebling, which occurred on the 22d. inst. . . . in the city of Brooklyn, New York, is an event full of sadness and sincere grief to the stockholders and directors of this company.

"Mr. Roebling, during his long connection with this company as chief engineer, always commanded in the highest degree the confidence and respect of its officers and stockholders. Known to most of us personally, his plain unostentatious manners and habits, his simple tastes, his noble and generous social qualities, were such as to win our esteem and love. He was, in all that he professed and did, an earnest, sincere man. He calculated to a hair's breadth his capacity for his work and made no mistakes. No better evidence of this is needed than a statement of the fact that in the work of constructing our bridge, lasting through a period of several years and where much of the work was of a new and dangerous character and had to be performed by men unskilled, not a single accident, mistake, or miscalculation was chargeable to him . . .

"His last complete great work at our city will stand for centuries a public benefaction and monument to his genius. . . ."

In the spirit of public service, the Bridge Company made contributions to local charities and to civic enterprises, such as the expositions which were held during this period. An all-time record was set for floods in February, 1883, when the river reached a height of over sixty-six feet. At this time the company assisted the relief work with its contributions for flood sufferers.

One year later, in February, 1884, a new flood record was established as the river rose to a height of over seventy-one feet. It was impossible for the ferry boats to land on either shore, even if they could have made their way across the rushing water. There was no other way of crossing but by the bridge. As the river continued to mount, the importance of the bridge became more apparent than ever before. If it could be kept open, fire protection, medical, and relief service could be extended to the cities of northern Kentucky. If not, the suffering in those isolated cities might be incalculable.

Long before the crest of the flood was reached on St. Valentine's Day, the icy water was sweeping around the entrance to the bridge. To maintain communications, Colonel Shinkle obtained a force to build flatboats. A number of these boats were speedily constructed in Cincinnati, for use between the end of the bridge and the shore of the flood. They were flatboats, with benches for passengers, managed by two or three men with iron-spiked poles. When put into operation, they were poled from the bridge just below the entrance on Front Street, against the current up to Walnut Street, and then up Walnut until they came to rest where the cobbled pavement sloped out of the water. A saloon just outside the reach of the flood there took its name, the Landing Saloon, from the landing of the boats at its door. Throughout the week of this flood, constant communication was thus maintained between the two sides of the river.

Other problems, less spectacular, required day-to-day attention to maintain smooth, regular service. Because of the steep grade at the bridge entrances, heavy wagons and carts, and sometimes even street cars, were occasionally stalled, and bridge attendants had to be ready to help them along and prevent blockades. When bicycles became popular in the 1880's, they were another problem to be met in the slow-moving mass of traffic.

At the end of 1879 the secretary notified the

Board of City Commissioners "that the steam cars and engines are in the habit of running on Front Street at all hours day and night to such an extent as to seriously incommode public travel and at times to make it dangerous to street cars and other vehicles." It took many years of negotiation before this problem was finally solved.

Although the bridge was finished in 1867, no institution of public service can ever be regarded as complete. The company discovered that constant attention was required to keep the bridge in the best condition. The pavements at the bridge approaches, having been laid down in cold weather, warped in the heat of summer, and in time had to be replaced. The sidewalk flooring became worn under the feet of thousands of persons a day, and the oak planks were replaced with cedar. Railings and other parts of the bridge demanded periodic coats of paint to preserve them.

One of the biggest tasks of the time was the maintenance of the bridge anchors. In the fall of 1892, the engineer reported on the subject: "The cable end of the southeast abutment was uncovered last summer to ascertain the condition of the wires inside of the masonry. At the point of connection with the anchor chain the cable is divided into twenty-eight strands looped around the two connecting pins. The outside wires of these strands were found to be badly oxydized by contact with the damp mortar in which they were imbedded, whilst the inside wires were not seriously injured. The loss of strength of the cable by reason of this deterioration was roughly estimated to be one-eighth of its original strength. It was then decided to restore the cable to its original strength and to preserve it, if possible, from further damage." This work was completed before the end of the year.

The opening of the two important railroad depots in Covington, the Kentucky Central and the Chesapeake and Ohio, made something of a boom in bridge traffic. Freight was unloaded in Kentucky, placed on wagons, and transhipped by way of the bridge to Cincinnati. For a few years the bridge prospered to such an extent that the company hoped it might begin paying dividends on the nonpreferred as well as the preferred stock.

Finally, when the dividends for the past quarter were declared on January 1, 1889, a dividend of one-half of one per cent on the nonpreferred stock was declared payable on demand. It was the only time in more than fifty years that the nonpreferred stock yielded a return. On September 1, 1889, the Chesapeake and Ohio opened its own bridge across the river. A large part of the freight hauled across the Suspension Bridge was now diverted to the new structure, and revenues and dividends fell off accordingly. Almost exactly two years later, on August 29, 1891, the Central Bridge was opened between Cincinnati and Newport. The income of the Suspension Bridge fell off still further.

A few months after the first quarter century of the bridge came to a close, death came to the man who was longest and most closely associated with its fortunes—Colonel Amos Shinkle. He died Sunday evening, November 13, 1892, in Covington, Kentucky. There he had lived for almost fifty years. As a businessman in the far-off days of President Polk, as a servant of public security during the great Civil War, as president of the School Board, as president of the First National Bank and the Covington Gas Light Company, he had served his city well for many years. Its churches and charities were memorials to his generosity. At his death the Bridge Company offered him this tribute:

"He was the unfaltering friend of the Suspension Bridge from its inception to its completion. In the dark days of its construction when friends failed, disappointments multiplied, and among its projectors many wavered and most of them despaired of success—then it was that the strong will and sublime faith of Mr. Shinkle rose to the occasion, and with words of fixed determination he declared that the bridge should be built. And built it was, and opened to the public on January 1, 1867. From that day until his death Mr. Shinkle's was the leading and guiding mind which directed the business and management of the company; and this he did with discretion, wisdom, and to the best interests of the enterprise...."

GATEWAY TO THE SOUTH

INTO THE TWENTIETH CENTURY

TOWARD the end of 1889 the Bridge Company began to consider the question of having electric lights at the bridge entrance. They were something of a novelty, and there were many objections to them. They were not adopted; but the discussion was a straw in the wind.

A few weeks later the company received a letter from E. F. Abbott, president of the Covington and Cincinnati Street Railroad Company. Abbott asked "on what terms the company would be allowed to cross the bridge, with cars operated by electricity, and put up and maintain the necessary poles and wires on the bridge." Horse-drawn street cars were on the way out and the world was rushing toward an age of electricity.

With the final passing of the horsecar in 1895 the bridge abruptly became obsolete. The two or three hundred crossings a day of the old, slow-moving cars could be handled easily. To take care of a thousand heavy high-speed electric cars a day made far heavier demands than the bridge was prepared to meet.

In 1895 and 1896, to keep up with the new requirements, the bridge was entirely rebuilt. During the former year new anchorages were constructed beyond the old anchor piers, and the brick and cement turrets were removed from the tops of the towers. The towers themselves were then prepared to receive the saddles, and stairways were built up for the workmen.

The spinning of the cables was begun in the spring of 1896; but because of delay in receiving the steel saddles and other equipment the construction was partially interrupted for more than four months. Meanwhile new tracks were being laid across the bridge for the electric street cars. The new anchor piers were finished, those in Covington above the level of the old piers and next to them; in Cincinnati below the old ones. Anchor plates were installed of about the same weight as the original plates, and the new steel cables attached. Instead of two cables supporting the bridge, there were now four, two on each side, and the strength of the bridge was more than doubled. The level of the roadway was also raised, made almost twice as wide, and by the end of the year the rebuilding of the bridge was complete. The Cincinnati approach was lengthened from Front to Second Street. In addition to the convenience of an easier slope, the higher level of this terminus brought it out of reach of many floods.

Another sign of the changing times appeared just after the turn of the century. In July, 1901, the first rates for automobiles were fixed. Unlike the change to electric street cars, the change from carriage to automobile traffic had little effect on

BRADFORD SHINKLE
President, 1892-1909

the bridge. No alteration in the physical equipment, such as laying new tracks, was necessary. The increased strength of the bridge, since the addition of two new steel cables to the two old ones of wrought iron was more than enough to carry all the motor traffic which could be loaded on the structure.

In another year the old Welsbach gas lamps were abandoned, and the first electric lights for the bridge were installed on the Covington and Cincinnati approaches. With the gradual extension of electric lighting after 1902, the broad arch of the bridge came to be as fascinating by night as by day.

During these years of transition, while the bridge was being made over from old to new, the president of the company was Bradford Shinkle. Only son of Amos Shinkle, he was elected to the Board of Directors December 17, 1883. Nine years later, on the death of his father, he became president. The virtual reconstruction of the bridge structure was accomplished during his administration. In later years, he traveled in California and Florida for his health; but like his father he was in Covington at the time of his death, May 7, 1909. His son, A. Clifford Shinkle, succeeded him as ninth president of the Bridge Company, the third of the family in that office, and the third president since the opening of the bridge.

A number of minor tasks first confronted the new president. During 1904, in 1908-1909, and again in 1913 the entire bridge was repainted. The Cincinnati approach was paved with granite blocks and the Covington with brick in 1911, at the same time that new street-car rails were laid down. The entire footwalk on both sides of the bridge was renewed with cedar and pine during 1914-1915.

Electrolysis on the bridge threatened to become a serious problem in 1902-1903, and again in 1912-1913. Engineers made a careful investigation and discovered the chief problem at the Covington approach. Electricity was escaping there from the street-car tracks into the bridge. The leakage was, however, slight, and the situation was corrected without much trouble.

The story of the bridge can never be far from the story of the river it spans. As it was the barrier of the river which called for the bridge a century before, it was now the same barrier which in 1913 called for the remaking of the bridge.

In March and April, 1913, the most disastrous flood on the Ohio in a quarter of a century, and the highest since 1884, suddenly swept down on the city. The streets at the Cincinnati end of the bridge were under water, yet the emergency required that they be kept passable. In this necessity a trestle bridge was built, stretching from the bridge approach east on Second Street to Walnut, and north on Walnut until dry land was reached.

Fortunately this makeshift served the purpose, but at the next meeting of the directors steps were

A. Clifford Shinkle
President, 1909—

immediately taken to carry the bridge approach to a still higher level. During 1913 and 1914 property was acquired piece by piece, and plans were drawn up for the extension of the bridge. Early in 1915, $600,000 in bonds was issued "to provide funds with which to refund the outstanding bonds, $283,000 of them, and to extend the present bridge structure from Second Street to Third Street in Cincinnati, Ohio, so as to protect the Cincinnati approach to the bridge against any future flood. . . ."

At length all the preparations were completed. In the spring of 1916 the concrete footings for the new extension were poured between Second Street and Third. The iron work was begun by the American Bridge Company in September. By mid-November a large part of it was finished. The new approach was finally opened in the fall of 1918.

The value and success of this extension was thoroughly demonstrated nineteen years later in the great flood of 1937. Then for the first time in any major flood the Cincinnati entrance was completely secure and above water. The only further change came in 1920-1921, when an additional street-car entrance was provided over Third Street to the Dixie Terminal Building. The first street cars were run into the Dixie Terminal in October, 1921.

THE BRIDGE TODAY

DURING the 1920's a complete reorganization was made of the capital structure of the Bridge Company. Ever since 1865 the capital consisted of $750,000 in preferred and $500,000 in nonpreferred stock. Of the old stock, only $413,300 had been sold; $86,700 was never issued. In 1925 the Board of Directors recommended making one class of stock instead of the two which then existed, and the issuing of $1,855,400 of capital stock. This figure was the valuation placed upon the bridge by the Supreme Court in 1890. The present holders of both preferred and nonpreferred stock were then to exchange their stock, share for share, for the new common stock.

After the exchange of stock was effected, the preferred and nonpreferred stock was canceled and the company declared a stock dividend of one hundred per cent. The holders of the stock were thus given double the number of shares they previously held.

When the capital structure was changed and the preferred and nonpreferred stock retired, it was discovered that the Bridge Company had about seventy-five lost stockholders. Since before the Civil War, the old nonpreferred stock had never paid dividends, the men who had bought it gradually came to consider it worthless. Years passed, and the earnings of the bridge never rose high enough to pay dividends on it. Only once, in 1889, one-half of one per cent was paid. Immediately afterward, with the opening of other bridges, traffic and earnings fell off. The old stock was put into attics and cellars and forgotten. Some of it, no doubt with a sigh, was thrown away. It passed from hand to hand, from father to son, until somewhere along the line the owners forgot that they had the paper around.

With the issuing of new common stock in 1925 this old stock was converted into a good investment. Much of it was quickly uncovered and exchanged. But several years later there were still, according to the old stock books, almost fourscore subscribers who had paid for and received stock, and had disappeared with it.

The story of finding these lost stockholders is as romantic as anything in the history of the bridge. A secretary who had worked for a trust company handling bridge affairs became familiar with the problem. On leaving the trust company, the idea of hunting these stockholders appealed to her, and she offered to try to locate them.

One of the lost owners was the Buena Vista Stone Company. Before the Civil War it had been paid partly in stock for supplying sandstone for the masonry. There seemed to be no trace of the company at all now that its bridge stock had become valuable. One day a tiny village was discovered far up the Ohio River bearing the suggestive name, Buena Vista. At the town there was not a trace of the company.

But in near-by Portsmouth, the court house held many old records. There, after a long search, the company was identified. According to the records it had gone into receivership many years before. It was then reorganized, and went on as the Buena Vista Stone Company. The new company continued for some years, until it, in turn, went into the hands of receivers. In that instance, the receivers wound up the business, sold all the assets, and closed it out.

Then the Bridge Company came along with this stock for which it could find no owners. Here it discovered too many. The matter was taken before a judge. Which stone company, the old or new, or what third party owned the stock? An administrator was appointed for the receivership and the case was reopened. At the end of this search a considerable block of stock was restored to its rightful owner.

Among the lost stockholders was an address, The Scioto Furnace Company. On the Bridge Company stock books was the record of a subscription and payment. The stock certificates had been issued; where were they? The furnace company was nowhere in existence.

Common sense suggested the Scioto Valley as the most likely place to search, and the detective-secretary got in her car and set off for Columbus.

Aerial View of the Flood of 1937

There she began systematically going through court-house records. Not a word about the furnace company was found. Slowly, she worked down the Scioto Valley, county by county. At every court house she stopped to read old deeds and registers. Nowhere was there a clue.

Near Portsmouth, at the end of the valley, she was ready to give up when she met a gray-bearded old man at a country filling station. He looked like an oldtimer; perhaps he had heard of the company? She asked him. The Scioto Furnace Company? He thought a moment, and answered, "Yes, there was once a company by that name not far from Portsmouth."

Some time later the detective-secretary was at the First National Bank in Portsmouth, asking for the president. He was busy at a directors' meeting; but she would wait. When the president came out she explained her purpose to him. Together they went back to the directors' room, and the secretary was introduced to the members of the board. One of them had an aunt, ninety-three years old, who might remember something about the company. He telephoned his aunt at once and made an appointment for lunch. At noon the four of them ate together, the director and his aunt, the president, and the secretary. When the excitement died down, the secretary asked the old lady about the Scioto Furnace Company.

"Give me fifteen minutes," she said. "It takes a little time to recollect." Before fifteen minutes had passed the whole story flooded back to her memory, and out it came. It was a long time since the company had disappeared. The owner had moved to Georgia, and there he had died. Perhaps he had left a family there. Some weeks later the secretary made a trip to Savannah, and there, sure enough, was the man to whom this bridge stock now belonged.

Another stockholder was discovered by a coincidence of names. One of the original companies contracting to supply materials for the bridge had, like others, been paid partly in stock. Later, it completely disappeared. In a Western State there was a little town which bore the rather odd name of one of the partners in the company. An investigation showed that the village had taken its name from the family, and descendants still lived in the neighborhood. Among them was found the owner of this forgotten stock.

In another instance, identity of names proved to be somewhat embarrassing. A Cincinnati attorney discovered that his grandfather had subscribed for and owned some of the old bridge stock. The stock certificates disappeared in the course of time, so that there was no way to prove the case conclusively. However, bond was given for it, and new stock certificates issued. These the attorney proceeded to sell, and subsequently divided the proceeds.

Then one day a letter came from Italy. The executor of an estate in Rome was inquiring whether the old stock of the Bridge Company was of any value. Gradually the story came out. The

THE OHIO BRIDGE

Aerial View of the Flood of 1937—Looking East

widow of an Italian wine merchant in Cincinnati had gone back to Rome and died there, leaving among her effects the original certificates of stock which were thought to have been lost. The woman was the granddaughter of the old stock subscriber, a man whose name was identical with that of the Cincinnati attorney's grandfather, but quite a different person.

Another stockholder, descendant of one of the original contractors, was discovered running a newspaper in Texas. He proved one of the hardest problems of all, for he refused a long time to accept the stock, insisting there was no Santa Claus.

In one way or another the lost stockholders were gradually found. Through correspondence long gathering dust, by the records of mossy tombstones, from yellowing wills and deeds, with the accidental hints of the map, and the unexpected recollections of old folk, they have been traced down one by one. The search is still going on. More than sixty have been located. At the latest count there are still twelve whose stock and dividends are being held in a bank, waiting the day when the hard work, ingenuity, and luck of the detective will restore it to them.

The most outstanding service rendered by the bridge in its three-quarters of a century was its performance during the Great Flood in 1937. With hundreds of thousands of persons depending on that one vital link, it was kept at the highest peak of effectiveness. The achievement of the men who maintained this service ranks with the finest work in the most terrible catastrophe of the Ohio Valley.

Throughout the whole month of January, 1937, constant rains drenched the Appalachians and turned the fields north of the Ohio into huge ponds. Early in the month the river was far higher than normal. On the morning of January eighteenth, when the river reached flood stage of fifty-two feet, it was the first January flood in ten years. Instead of coming to a peak and subsiding, the river now proceeded to rise higher and faster hour by hour for three days, until on Friday afternoon, January twenty-second, still in the midst of heavy rain, it broke every flood record in a century and a half. Then it began to slow down.

This was no ordinary flood. With thousands of acres under water in both Cincinnati and the Kentucky cities, tens of thousands of persons were homeless. Schoolchildren were dismissed early on Friday, some to help in flood work, others to reach home before street-car service might be interrupted in low-lying sections. How long the flood might last, no one could tell. It was already the worst in the city's experience; and the January rainfall, four times above normal, gave no sign of stopping.

Saturday morning the river was just over seventy-two feet high. It was still rising, but it was no longer rushing upward four inches an hour; lt was barely creeping up half an inch hourly.

Other bridges along the Ohio were already closed, blocked by the unprecedented high water. The Cincinnati end of the Suspension Bridge was high and safe; but the Covington approach was threatened by water coming up Second Street toward the bridge entrance. Saturday morning workmen began to build a dam across the street, blocking off the whole open space between the buildings on either corner. Sandbags, cement sacks, sand and gravel were piled all day long into a heavy dyke. By evening it was raised to a height of four feet six inches above the approach to the bridge. It was more than enough to protect the approach against any further rise which might be expected.

All day Saturday the river held its level, a little over seventy-two feet. Having broken all records, perhaps it would go down now. Hopeful watchers from time to time announced a drop in the stage. Late Saturday evening all doubts were erased. Once more the river began its terrifying march upward, undermining buildings, driving people from their homes. Already more than twice its normal width, the river now spread destruction over huge new areas for every foot it rose. Every inch now represented a far more tremendous volume of water than before. A little bit faster every hour Saturday night the river rose.

When Sunday morning dawned (if it could be

called a dawn when no sun shone), it heralded a Black Sunday which Cincinnatians would never forget. Heavy rains were beating down on a six-inch snowfall, and the river went wild. Mill Creek Valley, already a vast lake with islanded buildings disappearing one after another in the water, was the scene of tremendous fires at the Crosley Radio and Standard Oil plants. Electric power was rationed, telephone service curtailed, water cut off, street cars stopped, and then electric power came to an end altogether.

Saturday night, Sunday morning, Sunday afternoon, faster and faster the river roared upward and on. In Covington the bridge superintendent knew on Sunday morning that his dam would never give the necessary protection to the vital highway. Water was coming up side streets from every direction. Up Second Street from the west, up the lanes and through yards from the river, and up Greenup Street on the east it was closing in. One inch higher an hour brought it several feet closer to the bridge entrance; two inches, three higher an hour, and it came yards closer to the bridge; four inches, and five inches upward an hour the river mounted as it passed the seventy-six-foot stage.

At four o'clock Sunday afternoon the superintendent decided to build a causeway from the bridge to the highest land adjoining. With streets under water for blocks around, workmen began the construction of a ramp. It led diagonally from the bridge just south of the anchor wall

Covington in the Great Flood of 1937

across the office lawn and through a vacant lot to a point on Greenup Street several hundred feet away.

Sand and gravel bags, with a dirt fill, were used to build up a solid roadway. Through the icy, soaking rain three hundred men were kept busy Sunday evening piling up the sand and gravel. Clothing, food, and equipment were supplied to them on the spot. That evening water entered the bridge office at the corner of Court and Second, only a few feet from where the men were feverishly piling up the road. Office records and equipment and headquarters were hastily transferred to the home of the late Senator Ernst. On the other side of the causeway, the area between it and the old dam across Second Street was kept dry for the workmen by using pumps. Altogether five pumps were required to force the water over the embankment, back into the flooded territory below the approach.

As the river ceaselessly pushed its way up, the causeway was built to a height of three feet. All the sand and empty cement bags in Covington were used, and the river threatened to overtake the workmen. A desperate search was made for additional material. During the night trucks began hauling sand from Elmwood, north of Cincinnati, across the bridge for the built-up road. At one time forty trucks were hauling materials for this construction.

By two o'clock Monday morning the causeway was finished. It rose nearly seven feet above the level of the pavement. The old dam on Second Street was now useless. It could not even protect the men at work on the ramp. The pumps were pulled out, and the workmen withdrawn from the area. In a few hours the river broke through and came washing up the sides of the new causeway itself.

But there was as yet no limit to the flood, and all Monday morning the river continued to climb, inches every hour. More sand and gravel bags were brought from across the river. Soaking with the rain, they froze almost in the workmen's hands. Some who saw the glistening white film on the sacks rumored the bridge was being protected with dry ice! Two more feet were added to the height of the causeway before daybreak. A canteen was set up and the workmen given meals. There could be no thought of letting them leave the scene that day or the following night. Not until late on Tuesday morning did the flood turn from its crest and begin, ever so slowly, to subside.

The sand and gravel bags piled on the causeway were linked to keep them from washing out. Trucks passing back and forth over them acted as a roller, and bound them solidly together. Eventually a corduroy top was laid on the sandbags to keep further traffic from tearing them up. Altogether, by the time this road was completed early Tuesday morning, over thirteen hundred tons of sand, gravel, and dirt had been used. From the bridge to dry land in Covington a solid

Temporary Ramp in Covington—Flood of 1937

road had been built fifteen feet high, and continued in use from Monday, January 25, through the following Friday.

Lighting the bridge in the interest of safety was a problem in itself. When the tremendous upsurge of the river made it certain that the electric circuit would be flooded, workmen sealed the transformer to keep it watertight. Neither end of the bridge was out of power during the emergency. Feeding, clothing, and equipping the three hundred workmen employed was another task of great proportions. At the peak of the flood, one part of the Cincinnati approach over Front Street, passed forty inches below water. By using dykes and pumps, the roadway was kept dry, and few of those who crossed knew that they were traveling below the level of the flood there.

For more than a week, the Suspension Bridge was the only crossing kept open day and night for the service of the community.

From Steubenville to Cairo, the Suspension Bridge was the only crossing open on the Ohio River. Fire engines from Michigan and Illinois crossed here to go to the aid of cities in western Kentucky. Diesel engines and electric generating units for the hospitals of stricken Louisville passed over the Suspension Bridge. All the Red Cross workers from Northern cities took this route, the only route to Louisville, Paducah, and Memphis. One truckload after another of medicine and hospital equipment was rushed across to the prostrate communities below Cincinnati on the Ohio River.

Most important of all was the cry for food. Bread, meat, and vegetables were brought to the Cincinnati terminus of the bridge, and trans-shipped on light, mobile trucks to Kentucky and Tennessee.

In the whole history of the bridge, no story is more vivid than this telephone call at midnight from a city in the Bluegrass:

"Is the bridge open? Can trucks come through from Cincinnati?"

It was the mayor of Lexington calling. There was no bread in the city. Bread was needed for breakfast in Lexington—and it was there by morning.

The company has had many experiences, both good and bad. It has seen many changes come and go; but, taking affairs as they came, it has been a GOOD CROSSING.

THE OHIO BRIDGE

DIRECTORS OF THE BRIDGE COMPANY

1855
President, CHARLES STETSON

A. L. GREER WILLIAM S. JOHNSON
J. T. LEVIS J. R. WILLIAMS
J. D. PATCH (successor to W. S. Johnson)
AMOS SHINKLE (successor to J. D. Patch)

1856-1858
President, RICHARD H. RANSON
(Mar., 1856—Nov., 1858)

Covington

AMOS SHINKLE
  (Feb., 1856—Mar., 1866)
JOHN W. FINNELL
  (Mar., 1856—Mar., 1860)
HENRY BRUCE
  (Mar., 1856—May, 1859)

Cincinnati

MILES GREENWOOD
  (Mar., 1856—Nov., 1858)
JOSEPH C. BUTLER
  (Mar., 1856—Apr., 1856)
THOMAS PHILLIPS
  (Mar., 1856—Aug., 1856)
WILLIAM MCCAMERON
  (Apr., 1856—Mar., 1857)
  (Replacing J. C. Butler)
JOSEPH C. BUTLER
  (Aug., 1856—Mar., 1858)
  (Replacing T. Phillips)
G. BRASHEARS
  (Mar., 1857—May, 1857)
  (Replacing W. McCameron)
DAVID GIBSON
  (May, 1857—Mar., 1858)
  (Replacing G. Brashears)
THOMAS SHERLOCK
  (Mar., 1858—Mar., 1860)
  (Replacing J. C. Butler)
S. W. POMEROY
  (Mar., 1858—Mar., 1859)
  (Replacing D. Gibson)

President *pro tem*, MILES GREENWOOD
(Nov., 1858)
President *pro tem*, HENRY BRUCE
(Nov., 1858—Mar., 1859)

Covington
NAPOLEON B. STEPHENS
  (Nov., 1858—Mar., 1861)
  (Replacing H. Bruce)

1859-1860
President, HENRY BRUCE
(Mar., 1859)
President, MILES GREENWOOD
(Mar., 1859—Mar., 1860)

Covington	*Cincinnati*

AMOS SHINKLE
  (Feb., 1856—Mar., 1866)
JOHN W. FINNELL
  (Mar., 1856—Mar., 1860)
NAPOLEON B. STEPHENS
  (Nov., 1858—Mar., 1861)
	THOMAS SHERLOCK
	  (Mar., 1858—Mar., 1860)
	HENRY BRUCE
	  (Mar., 1859—May, 1859)
	GEORGE K. SHOENBERGER
	  (Mar., 1859—Mar., 1860)

1860-1866
President, JOHN W. FINNELL
(Mar., 1860—May, 1862)

Covington	*Cincinnati*

AMOS SHINKLE
  (Feb., 1856—Mar., 1866)
JESSE WILCOX
  (Mar., 1860—May, 1862)
NAPOLEON B. STEPHENS
  (Nov., 1858—Mar., 1861)
WILLIAM ERNST
  (Mar., 1861—Jan., 1863)
  (Replacing N. B. Stephens)
	MILES GREENWOOD
	  (Mar., 1860—Mar., 1861)
	RUFUS KING
	  (Mar., 1860)
	R. B. BOWLER
	  (Mar., 1860—July, 1864)
	G. W. COFFIN
	  (Mar., 1861—Mar., 1862)
	  (Replacing M. Greenwood)
	PHILIP HEIDELBACH
	  (Mar., 1861—June, 1862)
	  (Replacing R. King)
	MILES GREENWOOD
	  (Mar., 1862—Mar., 1865)
	  (Replacing G. W. Coffin)

THE OHIO BRIDGE

President, JESSE WILCOX
(May, 1862—Mar., 1866)

Covington

AMOS SHINKLE
(Feb., 1856—Mar., 1866)
JOHN W. FINNELL
(May, 1862—Sept., 1863)
(Replacing J. Wilcox)
NAPOLEON B. STEPHENS
(Jan., 1863—Apr., 1871)
(Replacing W. Ernst)
DANIEL BANNING
(Sept., 1863—Jan., 1872)
(Replacing J. W. Finnell)

Cincinnati

THEODORE COOK
(Jan., 1863—Jan., 1872)
(Replacing P. Heidelbach)
THOMAS SHERLOCK
(July, 1864—Mar., 1867)
(Replacing R. B. Bowler)
GEORGE K. SHOENBERGER
(Mar., 1865—1879)
(Replacing M. Greenwood)

1866-1892
President, AMOS SHINKLE
(Mar., 1866—Nov., 1892)

Covington

JEREMIAH W. BANNING
(Mar., 1866—Jan., 1876)
NAPOLEON B. STEPHENS
(Jan., 1863—Apr., 1871)
DANIEL BANNING
(Sept., 1863—Jan., 1872)
JESSE WILCOX
(Apr., 1871—Feb., 1875)
(Replacing N. B. Stephens)
M. M. BENTON
(Jan., 1872—Jan., 1881)
(Replacing D. Banning)
VINCENT SHINKLE
(July, 1875—Dec., 1883)
(Replacing J. Wilcox)
JOHN F. FISK
(Jan., 1876—Feb., 1902)
(Replacing J. W. Banning)
HOMER HUDSON
(Jan., 1881—Sept., 1902)
BRADFORD SHINKLE
(Jan., 1884—Nov., 1892)

Cincinnati

THOMAS SHERLOCK
(July, 1864—Mar., 1867)
GEORGE K. SHOENBERGER
(Mar., 1865—1879)
THEODORE COOK
(Jan., 1863—Jan., 1872)
GEORGE K. PENDLETON
(Mar., 1867—Dec., 1883)
(Replacing T. Sherlock)
JAMES BUGHER
(Jan., 1872—1879)
(Replacing T. Cook)
DAVID SINTON
(Jan., 1879—Aug., 1900)
A. H. BUGHER
(1879—Jan., 1888)
MATTHEW HART
(Jan., 1884—Jan., 1895)
H. HANNA
(Jan., 1888—Jan., 1892)
WILLIAM C. BARE
(Jan., 1892—Feb., 1893)

THE OHIO BRIDGE

1892-1909
President, BRADFORD SHINKLE
(Nov., 1892—May, 1909)

Covington	Cincinnati
JOHN F. FISK (Jan., 1876—Feb., 1902)	DAVID SINTON (Jan., 1879—Aug., 1900)
HOMER HUDSON (Jan., 1881—Sept., 1902)	MATTHEW HART (Jan., 1884—Jan., 1895)
WILLIAM K. BENTON (Nov., 1892—Apr., 1897) (Replacing B. Shinkle)	WILLIAM C. BARE (Jan., 1892—Feb., 1893)
FRANK P. HELM (Apr., 1897—July, 1908) (Replacing W. K. Benton)	CHARLES P. TAFT (Apr., 1893—Jan., 1930) (Replacing W. C. Bare)
JONATHAN D. HEARNE (Apr., 1902—July, 1905) (Replacing J. F. Fisk)	W. A. PROCTOR (Jan., 1895—Apr., 1897) (Replacing M. Hart)
DANIEL C. HEMINGRAY (Oct., 1902—Oct., 1911) (Replacing H. Hudson)	WILLIAM K. BENTON (Apr., 1897—Apr., 1914) (Replacing W. A. Proctor)
CHARLES H. FISK (Oct., 1905—Nov., 1930) (Replacing J. D. Hearne)	CHARLES SCHMALSTIG (Jan., 1901—Feb., 1916) (Replacing D. Sinton)
CHARLES C. CHASE (July, 1908—July, 1936) (Replacing F. P. Helm)	

1909-
President, A. CLIFFORD SHINKLE
(May, 1909—)

Covington	Cincinnati
DANIEL C. HEMINGRAY (Oct., 1902—Oct., 1911)	CHARLES P. TAFT (Apr., 1893—Jan., 1930)
CHARLES H. FISK (Oct., 1905—Nov., 1930)	WILLIAM K. BENTON (Apr., 1897—Apr., 1914)
CHARLES C. CHASE (July, 1908—July, 1936)	CHARLES SCHMALSTIG (Jan., 1901—Feb., 1916)
J. A. JOHNSON (Jan., 1912—Jan., 1922) (Replacing D. C. Hemingray)	E. W. STRONG (Jan., 1915—) (Replacing W. K. Benton)
H. P COLVILLE (Nov., 1930—) (Replacing Charles H. Fisk)	C. H. REMBOLD (Apr., 1916—) (Replacing C. Schmalstig)

THE OHIO BRIDGE

Covington
EDWARD A. VOSMER
  (July, 1936—   )
  (Replacing Charles C. Chase)
S. D. ROUSE
  (Jan., 1922—   )
  (Replacing J. A. Johnson)

Cincinnati
ROBERT A. TAFT
  (Jan., 1930—   )
  (Replacing Charles P. Taft)

www.ingramcontent.com/pod-product-compliance
Lightning Source LLC
Chambersburg PA
CBHW020122130526
44591CB00032B/345